MW01485476

EVER A SOLDIER

Reflections of a Veteran - From Horse Cavalryman to WWII to Vietnam

BY LILLY ROBBINS BROCK

EVER A SOLDIER

Copyright © 2017 Lilly Brock

All rights reserved. No part of this publication may be reproduced, distributed, or transmitted in any form or by any means, including photocopying, recording, or other electronic or mechanical methods, without the prior written permission of the publisher, except in the case of brief quotations embodied in reviews and certain other non-commercial uses permitted by copyright law.

Although the author and publisher have made every effort to ensure that the information in this book was correct at press time, the author and publisher do not assume and hereby disclaim any liability to any party for any loss, damage, or disruption caused by errors or omissions, whether such errors or omissions result from negligence, accident, or any other cause.

Official Website: http://www.lillyrobbinsbrock.com

DEDICATION

To my father, a World War II veteran, and every other veteran who has stepped forward to protect and serve our country, the United States of America.

"All the great things are simple, and many can be expressed in a single word: freedom, justice, honor, duty, mercy, hope."
~ Winston Churchill

TABLE OF CONTENTS

FOREWORD

✦✦✦✦

I'd like to think my dad is smiling down at me. He passed on in 1994, and I miss him dearly. He was a World War II veteran and my own personal hero. Recently, I found two letters written by him while he was on the battlefront of North Africa. His letters inspired me to find a veteran still living and tell his story. I found my veteran, Maury Hooper, and told his story in my book *Wooden Boats & Iron Men*. Meeting Maury and writing his story has turned out to be one of the most rewarding things I've ever done. I'll always remember the joy the book brought to that PT sailor and his family. His story is preserved forever. As I reflect back, it is quite surreal to think about meeting a total stranger, learn about his entire life, and then, to become part of that life. I came to care about this man, and I believe he cared about me. After spending several months interviewing him, I finished the book and presented it to him in the presence of his family, friends and peers. Three weeks later at the age of ninety, Maury passed away. It would be nice to think that he and my dad have met.

Every veteran has a story, and so, I have continued on to write another soldier's story. This World War II veteran is ninety-nine years young. Meet Major Philip Edward Bishop. I marvel at what good physical shape he is in, and his mind is razor sharp. I said to him, "Phil, I've never talked to anyone who is at the age of ninety-nine." He smiled and said, "Well, I'm heading for the big one!" Phil will reach the milestone of one hundred years old in July of 2017.

It's interesting, as I have come to know Phil and see the contrast between his and Maury's life and personality—even the contrast in their war experience. Maury served in the South Pacific theater and Phil in the European theater. These two men and my dad are all woven from a common thread. They have true grit, and are part of the Greatest Generation which produced a generation of people made up of strength, tenacity, persistence and courage. It's my honor to bring another story of one of the many unsung heroes into the light.

"We and all others who believe in freedom as deeply as we do, would rather die on our feet than live on our knees."

~ Franklin D. Roosevelt

CHAPTER 1

A Close Call

✦✦✦✦

"Jesus! Someone just shot at me!"

On a rainy day in April of 1945, Lieutenant Philip Bishop and his sergeant stood atop a dike on the bank of the Mulde River. They were on one side of the river and the German troops were on the other. After being under heavy artillery fire in Remagen, Germany, the Lieutenant had received orders to advance toward Leipzig in East Germany to position his platoon along the Mulde River.

Philip had just heard a loud noise much like that of a whip being violently cracked, but it wasn't a whip. What he heard was the sound of a bullet flying past his head. He was lucky, snipers usually don't miss. There's an old saying, *It's the bullet you don't hear that will kill you.* The speed of the bullet actually breaks the sound barrier. A vacuum is created immediately behind the bullet resulting in a sharp crashing sound as it passes, caused by air closing in behind the bullet base.

They jumped down from the dike. Philip grabbed his field glasses and looked across the river to spot the shooter. He narrowed his search down to a two-story house, and said, "I see a rifle barrel—just the end of a rifle barrel sticking out of the window of that god damned house over there."

Lieutenant Bishop told the sergeant he was going to shoot a round toward the window to see what was going on. He took the regular shell out of his rifle and inserted a tracer shell. "I sited in on the target, and I raised it a couple of inches and squeezed one off. The tracer went straight into the window—straight in."

The next day, another company of soldiers showed up looking for their officers who had come down the day before to pass through Lieutenant Bishop's lines. The officers were drunk. Lieutenant Bishop's men had warned them that there were Germans over there, but they replied, "We're just looking around." Since Philip's men were only privates, they didn't try to stop the officers. Three went through the lines, but only one returned. The entire company planned to cross the bridge to look for the two missing officers. Philip said to them, "Lord only knows where they could be. They could be dead in the first place, and in the second place, it's been a day. They could be in eastern Germany by now." Then he pulled one of the privates aside, and said, "Do you see that house over there? If you get there, and find the house, check the upstairs, will you?"

When the company returned, Philip found the private and asked him if he was able to check the upstairs in the house. The private said, "Yah! There's a dead German up there."

No surprise. Philip Bishop was a dead shot. He had been shooting a gun since he was seven years old in Lewiston Orchards in Idaho.

CHAPTER 2

The Best Poacher

◆◆◆◆

Nine-year-old Philip was obsessed with hunting, and living in Lewiston, Idaho, offered him ample opportunity. His father owned a .22 Winchester pump-action rifle, and being aware of his son's obsession, hid the rifle. When Philip realized the rifle was missing, he searched the entire property until he found it. He felt victorious when he discovered it hidden out in the barn complete with a box of shells. His parents worked in an apple packing plant at the time, which gave him complete freedom when he came home from school in the afternoon until six in the evening. "I became a self-taught gunman, but not before shooting a hole in the porch floor the first time I loaded the gun," Philip said.

Pheasants were plentiful in Lewiston Orchards, so he decided to bag some. He didn't get any pheasants, but he did draw the attention of an unhappy neighbor. The neighbor didn't waste any time to tell Philip's parents about their son who was shooting up the neighborhood. Philip's father took the gun away from him, and hid it again. Young Philip wasn't about to settle, and was determined to find the gun. He searched for two days until he found it. His hunting days were back.

Once again, the same neighbor knocked on the Bishop's door and complained about Philip. The neighbor was concerned that he and his family's lives were in danger. Philip's father knew he needed to try something different with his son. He made a deal with Philip that if he would give up rifle hunting, he would get him a shotgun for Christmas. His father reasoned that a .410 shotgun would only cause harm at close range whereas a .22 rifle could cause damage up to a mile away. That sounded like a good deal to Philip, and his father kept his word. Now Philip had his own weapon and was free to resume hunting pheasant. Soon he was contributing to his family's meals, and to his neighbor's meals as well. The neighbor was pleased, and in return, gave Philip a box of shells.

When Philip was twelve years old, his parents gave him a small rat terrier dog which he named Spot. Spot turned out to be excellent at pheasant hunting. When Spot's rear end wiggled, Philip knew his dog was on to the scent of a pheasant. One day, Philip shot a pheasant, but by only wounding it, the pheasant kept running. Spot was excited and on impulse, ran after it. In all the flurry, Spot ran under Philip's hunting partner's steel-toed boots causing his partner to accidentally kick the dog's head. Spot died instantly. Philip gave Spot a tearful funeral and buried him in an old badger hole. His dog was his best friend, and the loss was so upsetting he didn't hunt again for a month.

"By age fourteen, I was an accomplished wing shot and the pheasant population suffered considerably." Lewiston Orchards had been designated as a game preserve. There were rules and hunting seasons. That didn't matter to Philip. For the next few years, he hunted whenever and wherever he wanted. Philip boasted, "I was young, but I was one of the best poachers in the entire area, and proud of it." People turned him in, but it didn't stop him. The local game warden, who was aware of Philip's poaching activities, warned him about the rules he needed to follow. Philip said, "It was like telling a cat not to hunt mice."

One time Philip was turned in to the authorities and he ended up in court. He had emptied his shotgun into a flock of ducks sitting in a lake that happened to be in the middle of a game preserve. He had been turned in by a man who hated the Bishops. Particularly, Philip's grandfather (on his mother's side) who had come to the aid of the man's wife. This man had a habit of beating his wife. The man knew he would be no match to beat up Philip's grandfather. His grandfather spent his life as a mule skinner driving a wagon and was a tough man. During the court proceeding, Philip was ready to face the witness who turned him in, but for some reason the man said, "I didn't actually see Philip shoot the ducks." Philip was shocked since he knew the man heard him shooting. The man was milking his cow and when he heard the shots, raised up and saw Philip shooting at the ducks. He was only about thirty feet away. Years later, Philip admitted to his father that he actually did shoot at the ducks. Then, his father told Philip about his visit to the man's house informing him that if his son was convicted, he should be prepared to receive a sound beating.

By the time Philip was eighteen, he had received several stern lectures from several game wardens. His father was aware of Philip's violations and decided it was time for a serious talk with his son. Philip agreed to try harder to obey the law. All was well until a cute little redheaded girl and her family moved into the neighborhood. When she informed him she had never eaten pheasant, Philip, with an air of confidence, assured her that he would be happy to take care of that problem in no time at all.

The following day, he visited the game preserve and shot two pheasants, but a persistent game warden who was determined to catch him in the act, caught him red-handed. Philip reflected back to his father's warning about what could happen if he were caught, and now he was caught. He had to appear in court before the judge who fined him twenty-five dollars—a lot of money in those days. Since Philip's father worked in the courthouse, Philip assumed his father would show up for the hearing, but his father was nowhere in sight. He scanned the room a second time. *Where's my father? Am I to stand here alone?* When the judge issued the ruling, Philip said, "I don't have any money." He thought perhaps the judge would simply warn him and tell him not to do it again. Instead, he told Philip to go upstairs and report to the sheriff, and said, "You can serve it at a dollar a day." With shoulders slumped and head lowered, Philip slowly climbed the stairs to the jail area thinking his father would surely show up and rescue him. But he didn't. The sheriff, who knew Philip, said "You're here to stay with me, I suppose." Philip responded, "I'm afraid so." The sheriff let him stand around for about a half hour. Then he said, "Your father paid your fine earlier today, so get the hell out of here." Philip's poaching days were over.

CHAPTER 3

The Year 1917

✦✦✦✦

On a summer day in July of 1917, a baby boy entered the world. Philip and Clara Bishop were thrilled when he came along. They never thought they would have children. They named him Philip Edward, Jr., and he would be their only child. The family lived in a neighborhood called Lewiston Orchards in Lewiston, Idaho.

When Philip Edward, Jr. was born, Idaho had been a state for only twenty-seven years. There were men still living who could tell personal stories about the Nez Perce Indian, Chief Joseph, on the battlefield; and other men who reminisced about their days of working on the railroads in the 1870s and 1880s. Women proudly talked about casting their first vote after Idaho granted them that right in 1896 even though the Nineteenth Amendment had not been ratified by the federal government, and wouldn't happen until 1920. Indians still pitched tents, Idaho became famous for her *Idaho potatoes*, and automobiles made their appearance. Idahoans had a strong sense of community. They enjoyed their county fairs and church socials, spelling bees, sleigh rides in the winter, celebrating the Fourth of July, small town baseball, rabbit and pheasant hunting, and salmon fishing in Idaho's Salmon River.

On April 6th, three months before Philip's birth, the United

States entered into the Great War (World War I). Although the United States tried to remain neutral when the Great War began overseas in 1914, it performed an important role of supplying raw materials and money to Great Britain and the other Allied powers. During this time, the farmers and ranchers flourished. They were encouraged to increase their production to aid the war effort. This proved to be a great opportunity for the farmers and ranchers since they enjoyed being able to sell their products at unprecedented prices. But the increased production caused a labor shortage, so the Idahoans rallied. Businessmen volunteered, judges postponed civil cases that required a jury until after the planting and harvest season, and the schools proclaimed spring and fall vacations to free up the children to thin sugar beets and pick potatoes.

Inevitably, the United States entered the war. President Wilson endeavored to maintain the nation's neutrality, but he could no longer ignore the impending threats of the German Empire. On May 7, 1915, the British ocean liner, *Lusitania,* was torpedoed by a German submarine. Within minutes, the vessel sank with 128 American souls on board who lost their lives. Another concern was the discovery on January 19, 1917, of a secret telegram sent from the German Foreign Minister, Arthur Zimmerman, to the Mexican leader. The British naval intelligence intercepted and decrypted the message, which consisted of an invitation for Mexico to join Germany as its ally against the United States. As compensation, Germany would send money and assistance to Mexico to help it recover the United States territories of Texas, New Mexico and Arizona that it lost during the Mexican-American War seventy years earlier. The British forwarded the *Zimmerman Telegram* to President Wilson the following month, February. There was also the unchecked aggression of German submarines attacking American merchant ships, and finally, succeeding in sinking seven U.S. ships in

February and March of 1917. On April 16, 1917, the United States joined its allies—Britain, France and Russia, to fight in the Great War.

Americans nationwide united to support the war effort. Approximately four million men and women served in the Great War. America lost over 117,000 of her soldiers—some were killed in action and others died from disease. Included in the 117,000 deaths were 782 Idahoans. Americans on the home front did everything they could to support the war effort. Women worked in factories to replace the men who went to war. People rationed what they ate. The term *wheatless Mondays and meatless Tuesdays* was born. Women at home created recipes for sugarless, eggless, milkless, and butterless cakes. They gardened and organized canning clubs, and planted *victory gardens* to help provide food for the soldiers.

The American spirit was everywhere. At the Pocatello railroad stop, local women volunteered at a Red Cross canteen unit to serve soldiers who were on their way to the West Coast. The canteen provided service before and after the Armistice. In December of 1918, one month after Germany surrendered, the Pocatello canteen provided and served 500 gallons of coffee, 30,000 sandwiches and 30,000 doughnuts to returning soldiers.

Philip was just over a year old when the Spanish Flu epidemic reached Idaho in early October of 1918. Idaho's State Board of Health issued a statewide order effective on October 10, 1918, prohibiting all public assemblies. When a train or automobile passed through a town, the occupants weren't allowed to stop. Then on the eleventh hour of the eleventh day of the eleventh month in that year of 1918, the Great War ended. It became known as the *war to end all wars.* When Idahoans learned about the Armistice, they were ecstatic, and threw caution aside as they gathered to celebrate. The result was catastrophic. The flu was unstoppable and thousands became infected. Hospitals and their personnel were strained to the maximum. Businesses came to a standstill. Anyone who ventured outside was required to wear cotton gauze masks. The quarantines which included guarding each county's border, continued until March of 1919, when the pandemic finally came to an end. Idaho's Indian population was also affected. Out of the 4,208 Indians, there were 634 cases of influenza resulting in 72 deaths. And nationwide, the flu affected approximately twenty-five percent of the population.

While the farmers and ranchers experienced a short period of prosperity during the war, they were about to swallow a bitter pill after the war. Idaho's main industries of mining, farming, and timber were drastically affected by the fallout of the Great War. Unlike other parts of the nation, including the industrial east coast, they didn't enjoy the prosperity and gaiety of the *Roaring Twenties.* To curb the inflation that was raging, the Federal Reserve Board tightened credit in late 1919. Farm prices took a nosedive while the agricultural land lost value. The demand for Idaho minerals and lumber declined. Idahoans experienced an economic depression that continued through the 1920s. The price for Idaho potatoes that were once priced at one dollar and fifty-one cents a bushel in 1919, fell to thirty-one cents a bushel in 1922. This small depression, however, was only a prelude of what was about to come.

Philip Edward Bishop, Sr. was twenty-nine years of age when he became a father. He was handsome, brown-eyed, tall, and trim of carriage. He possessed a sharp mind and worked hard to provide for his family. He was known to be a man of integrity and believed in being accountable for his actions.

Clara Bishop was a petite and trim lady. She had large brown eyes, long brown hair which she wore in a braid around the top of her head like a tiara. While she was always ready to offer a warm generous smile, she was a woman of tenacity, and never wavered from her course of action despite any challenge in her path. Sometimes, according to those who knew her well, her strength resulted in a little bossiness.

Philip, Jr. spent his childhood in Lewiston Orchards in Idaho. It was a rural community of small farms several miles south of Lewiston. Lewiston Orchards came into being in 1905 when irrigated tracts for planting apple orchards were offered in all sections of the Northwest. The orchards consisted of several plots ranging in size from twenty up to one hundred acres. The Bishops owned forty acres. They grew cherries, alfalfa, lettuce, and rotating crops of potatoes.

The summers were hot, and the winters were mild. Because of the minimal rainfall in Lewiston Orchards, irrigation was necessary to supplement the lack of rain. The supply of water came from Craig Mountain where reserves were built to capture the water from the melting snows. Lake Waha was one of the sources of supply. At the highest point in Lewiston Orchards, there was also a storage reservoir consisting of three-thousand-acre-feet of water. This water was distributed through underground pressure pipes to all the users. The water was pure and remained uncontaminated. Prior to the irrigation solutions, the roads were hub deep with dust, and were impassable when it rained. To solve this problem, the farmers covered the roads with straw.

Lewiston Orchards had been planned to be an apple district. There were thousands of acres of apple orchards planted throughout the Northwest. In the beginning, as the orchards came into bearing, the farmers made a decent profit. But the industry became overdone, and only those who were situated for transporting their produce survived. Thus, the apple trees were pulled, and cherry trees took their place. Lewiston Orchards offered more than cherries. There was a variety of fruits and vegetables produced not found anywhere else in the same latitude in North America, including English walnuts, filberts, chestnuts, and Muscat and Malaga grapes.

Philip and his parents lived in a small one-bedroom house. Though the house was small, it contained the necessities. There was a small wood cook stove that accommodated a smoke-blackened coffee pot and a large well-used iron kettle. Nearby, there was a small wooden food safe where a water bucket and gourd dipper rested. A table with one chair and two wooden benches sat on the creaky bare wood floor, and the room was lit by a small kerosene wall lamp. There were wires strung across the room used to support curtains. Philip climbed a set of steep stairs up to the attic where he slept at night on a bedroll and a mass of quilts. The attic wasn't the most comforting place to sleep. Because there was no other escape route besides the stairs, it was a dangerous place to be if there was a fire.

The privy stood next to the side of the barn. It was made of unpainted, weathered, silver pine boards and resembled a vertical box with a slanted roof. The flimsy door was fastened from the inside with a large wooden button nailed onto the doorframe. Inside, one used the bench that was about three feet high with oval holes cut in each side of the seat. "The very shape of the holes informed one instantly of its function," said Philip. "A stack of newspapers, a box of corncobs and an old Sears Roebuck catalog sat on the floor providing a choice for *cleaning."*

Clara Bishop's day began before sunrise. After she cooked breakfast and cleaned the house, her regimen consisted of laundry, canning, and finally, preparing and serving dinner. After dinner, she washed the dishes by hand, and scrubbed the floor with hot water and lye.

Her pride and joy was her vegetable garden. She planted green beans, butter beans, peas, tomatoes, corn, squash, onions, potatoes, turnip greens, peppers, beets, radishes, carrots, and eggplant. Clara laid out the rows with geometric precision, and any weed that dared to make an appearance was immediately plucked. The yearly yield from her garden was plentiful, so the family seldom needed to buy food from the local grocery store.

The Bishops also raised chickens and hogs. Because there was no refrigeration or cold storage, the hog killing took place during the cold weather. It was critical to butcher the hogs when there were several days of continuous cold temperature to have adequate time to process and preserve the meat. Once they completed the process, they hung the hams and bacon in the attic after they were cured.

Philip's chores consisted of hoeing his mother's garden, cleaning the chicken pen, and milking the cow. He described his experience with the cow.

"In the half light of dawn, I pulled on my overalls, ran downstairs through the kitchen, grabbed the milking buckets with water for washing the cow's bags, and went to the barn. I mixed up her feed and put it in the cow's trough in the stall where she had been confined all night since milking time the evening before. While the cow munched and made chewing sounds, I bathed her teats, cleaning from them the waste encrusted there during a night of lying in it. I didn't like to milk her because she swung her *shitty* tail around, slapping me across the head and sometimes kicked the bucket over. I developed an early milking machine by pushing a straw up into her teats to let the milk run out. It worked well, until my father curtailed my method who said I would cause her an infection. So, I had to go to the regular way by sitting on my haunches with the milk bucket between my knees, and milk with both hands directly into the big heavy tin bucket—first the left hand and then the right hand--in a steady, strong and rapid rhythm."

Philip spent his first eight years of school at Lower Tammy grade school. The school building was an old wooden, unpainted two-story structure. Grades one through four were taught downstairs, and grades five through eight upstairs. The school was located just outside of Lewiston Orchards, which was about three miles away. Philip walked to school every day. Anyone who lived five or more miles away rode horses.

"I had a young teacher named Margie MacIntosh, who I thought was wonderful. She was the daughter of a rich farmer and lived near the school. I still remember one embarrassing incident. At noon, I was riding a horse that one of the girls rode to school since she lived five miles away. Her saddle had been wired together, and a piece of the wire hooked my crotch as I dismounted and ripped my pants. I didn't go back to class, and a boy told the teacher, 'Philip ripped his britches and he is out in the barn.' Miss MacIntosh came out with her needle and thread, and sewed my pants back together. I hated the whole affair."

Philip recalled learning a life lesson when he was in the first grade. He noticed a large iron pot in the classroom, which in his mind was just *sitting around*. Thinking it wasn't in use and didn't belong to anyone, he took it home to present the prize to his mother. She informed him that what he had done was called *stealing*. His mother told him to carry it back and put it where he found it.

When Philip was in sixth grade, he learned that sometimes life isn't always fair. "Another young lad kicked me in the rear. He took off with me right behind him, and when I couldn't catch up with him, I called him a bunch of names that *apparently* hurt the little girls' ears. 'Well, well, well!' the male teacher repeated. 'This calls for a paddling.' First, he removed his coat. 'Bend over that chair,' he directed as he took the paddle off the wall. As I bent over, I was frantic and looked for an avenue of escape. There was no way to run to freedom. The humiliating horror that I had avoided for six years was on me so suddenly that I had no time to dwell on it. I was about to get a whipping at school. He drew back the paddle and let go, again and again. The shock of the blows was so great I could hardly maintain my footing and the pain so intense that I thought I would scream aloud despite my resolve. When I went back to class and sat down, I was surprised to find that I couldn't feel the chair with my numb buttocks, although the entire area seemed to be on fire. And the worst thing about the whole incident was the other kid was not punished at all, not even a word."

Philip attended Lewiston High School at the age of twelve. He soon learned that the kids from Lewiston Orchards were considered *poor trash* by the more sophisticated *town* kids. High school was more challenging. Instead of being in the same room filled with different grade level students, he had to adjust to having only his grade level of about twenty students together in a room. He missed hearing the older classmates recite their lessons, and, since there were several students for the teacher to focus attention on, he had enjoyed unnoticed periods of time daydreaming. He was very happy to graduate from high school at the age of sixteen. "I was more than ready for life," said Philip.

During the summer, Philip found ways to earn money. He sacked potatoes, picked cherries, and stacked alfalfa. When the strawberries were ready, he picked for several farmers. The pay was twenty-five cents for a twenty-five- pound crate. If conditions were good, he made seventy-five cents to a dollar in an eight-hour day. By the time he was twelve years old, he had built up a *fortune* of over one hundred dollars in a bank account, but he didn't get to keep the money for long. His parents became desperate for money and emptied his account. Philip understood their desperation and knew they felt guilty for taking his hard-earned money. His parents carved out a living by raising cherries, lettuce, potatoes, and alfalfa. Even though the family worked hard and long hours for every dollar they earned, Philip always felt they all had a good life, and reflected, "Never once did I realize how poor we were. We were poor, but proud."

Christmas in the Bishop household was a lean time. The Bishops simply had no money. Philip recalled one Christmas when he wanted a bicycle, but he knew he had no chance of getting one since it was at the unreachable price of fifteen dollars. Then one day, he found a bicycle hidden under a piece of tin in a junk pile. His father assumed it had been stolen and immediately reported the discovery to the sheriff. The sheriff told Philip and his father to hold the bicycle for thirty days while he attempted to find the owner. "That was the longest thirty days," said Philip. After the waiting period was over, no one came to claim the bicycle. Philip was rewarded for his patience, and the prized bicycle was his.

Because gas was so expensive at seven cents a gallon, the family walked to their destination most of the time. Philip's father's first car was a two-seater 1917 Ford which ran off and on, and a flat tire became a daily occurrence. Learning to repair a flat tire was one of the first requirements of the driver.

On one occasion in 1923, Philip and his father took the car on a long road trip. It was a two-hundred-mile fishing excursion to the Salmon River. They experienced three or four flat tires on that trip. Then, when they drove down the Whitebird Mountain road, they had a thrill ride they would never forget. The brakes weren't working, so they had to slow their speed by using the lower and reverse gear to back down part of the road.

The mighty Salmon River, with its wellspring on the Continental Divide between central Idaho and southern Montana, flows westerly through the center of Idaho and empties into the Snake River where the states of Idaho, Washington and Oregon meet. This wild turbulent river is often called the *River of No Return* due to it being considered impossible to go upstream the length of the river by boat. The feat could be done by laboriously pulling, poling, rowing, and portaging a boat to propel it up the river, but it was such a difficult task, it was classed as impossible. Along the river, big game was in abundance and the side streams were stocked with game fish. During the spring run, hundreds of fishermen lined the banks, and many fishermen walked away with large catches. Using a cut willow pole, Philip caught twenty fish on their trip. On another trip, his folks and friends caught sixteen hundred trout which they smoked. Smoked trout hung in the Bishop's attic and contributed to many meals.

The Snake River flows along the border of Oregon and Idaho, emptying into the Columbia River along its path, and carves a one-hundred-mile deep trench across Idaho for nearly two hundred miles. This canyon, known as Hell's Canyon, is the deepest and most impressive gorge on the North American continent and is deeper than the Grand Canyon. Hikers on the Snake River trail would see numerous granite outgrowths and pass by steep descents plunging hundreds of feet to the river below. While hiking through the Hells Canyon Wilderness, one would experience a scene of cactus, vibrant wildflowers, wild chukar partridge, mule deer, bighorn sheep, and other wildlife.

Philip was drawn to this Idaho wilderness, and would always hold fond memories of his excursions and adventures he shared with his parents and friends.

CHAPTER 4

The Great Depression

◆◆◆◆

The year 1929 ushered in a devastating economic slump for Americans across the nation and countries worldwide. The Great Depression emerged in October of that year, and would not end until 1939. It all began with the catastrophic collapse of stock market prices on the New York Stock Exchange. The stock prices continued to fall, and by late 1932, dropped to about twenty percent of their original value in 1929. Fortunes were lost, and frantic people in the big cities jumped out of windows to their death. Investors were ruined, and many banks were forced into insolvency. Banks started calling in loans. Anyone who purchased a home or had anything on loan lost it all through repossessions. People became homeless. Unemployment tripled. Soup kitchens and bread lines were the norm for the city dwellers.

People living in the Pacific Northwest were slightly better off. They lived in a land of plentiful bounty. Besides their farm crops and orchards, fishing and hunting helped to sustain the families. Like California, Idaho became a destination for the Midwest migrators such as the *Okies* and *Arkies* which resulted in a surge of the state's population. This provided an opportunity for the creative Idahoans. They clear cut large portions of their land to sell to the migrants. Unfortunately, not all the land sold, and the once wooded acreage turned into unused acres of stumps.

Idaho, though, suffered the hardest of the Pacific Northwest states. Southern Idaho was suffering from severe drought, and the migrants who settled there added an additional burden to the already stressed situation. The migrants from the Great Plains states were running away from drought and dust conditions and thought they were moving to a safe haven. Those who settled in Southern Idaho during this time, must have been sorely disappointed when they found themselves back in the middle of drought conditions.

Farmers in Southern Idaho were struggling, especially those in the Snake River plains. From October of 1933 through April of 1934, the rainfall was sixty-five percent less than normal causing crop losses to potatoes, beans, beets, peas, and hay. Creeks and watering holes dried up which impacted the livestock.

There was a telegram to the Universal News Service in Chicago on July 26, 1934, in which Idaho Governor Ross declared:

> In Idaho the drought is serious, the worst in the history of the white man in this territory. Rivers and creeks are drying up which in previous years furnished irrigation. Thousands of springs that have been used for watering livestock in the mountains have become dry, and water must be furnished from other sections. While people in the affected areas will not be required to evacuate, feed must be shipped in to save the livestock....With assistance of the Federal Government, we will be able to sustain our people in their homes without evacuation.

Farm prices fell forty-four percent between 1929 and 1930. With prices falling, the farmers who still had crops, couldn't afford to harvest them. Ironically, food rotted in the fields while people elsewhere were starving.

When building came to a halt, there was no demand for lumber thereby affecting the timber industry. Mining was hit hard as well. Silver prices dropped in value from one dollar and thirty-nine cents to twenty-four cents in 1933.

Even though the Depression put a great strain on Idahoans, they managed to survive with their *can-do* attitude and willingness to work hard and to come together. They lived simply and believed in helping their fellow neighbor.

When people lost their property to the bank, Idahoans banded together to attend the local Sheriff's Auction to bid the lowest price possible on the particular property being auctioned off. If they won the bid, they duly paid the sum, and returned the property to its original owner. Not all the properties could be saved. Many of the Orchards residents lost their farms. Philip said, "Despite working twelve hours a day, our farm went back to the bank in 1934." With no place to live, Philip and his parents moved in with his grandfather, John Edward Bishop, who had been a widower since 1924.

In 1875, John Edward Bishop and his two brothers, Charles and Al, were among a handful of white men to settle in the Snake River Country. Indians lived there for centuries. The Bishop brothers left the *Show Me* State of Missouri and worked their way across the country and settled first in Pullman, Washington. Finally, they moved to the lower Snake River area for the year-round climate. John Bishop acquired his land by giving the Indian who was located there a ten-dollar piece to vacate the premises. One brother, Al Bishop, acquired 170 acres of adjoining land in the same year. John's older brother, Charles, claimed 169 acres along the river bar in 1884, giving the Bishop brothers a total of over 500 acres which became known in Whitman County as Bishop's Bar. Bishop's Bar was located about twenty-two miles from Lewiston, Idaho. Although steamers periodically went up and down the river, there were years when they saw almost no one but Indians. The brothers began with grain, but were determined to raise fruit. Another brother, William, who was the county auditor in Spokane, Washington, was supportive of their decision. The brothers experienced a lucky business venture in sheep which gave them an unexpected financial opportunity to begin their dream of planting fruit trees.

Philip described the land of his grandfather.

"Here where the cool, green water mirrored the steep bluffs and deep canyons gathered to the edges of the Snake, on sand bars that ran back to the foothills, the red men had for centuries made their camps. Soil along the bottoms was a mixture of river sand and volcanic ash. Outcroppings of basaltic rock and granite clung to the canyon walls.

"Along the north bank of the Snake River, under the towering hills that surrounded it, was Wawawai. Named by the Indians and originally spelled Wawawa (wa meaning talk), the word means council grounds."

In 1886, John E. Bishop at the age of 38, married the daughter of his neighbor, James Virgil O'Dell, the first attorney in Whitman County. James O'Dell had property above Granite Point. His daughter, Nora Fields O'Dell Bowman, was a young widow. John and Nora became the parents of six children, Philip Edward (Philip, Jr.'s father), John Alfred (Fritz), Margaret, James O'Dell (who died at the age of twenty-one of a throat infection), Charles Fields and Clarissa Frances.

In the early 1920's, John and Nora relocated to Lewiston Orchards. Nora died in 1924 at the age of sixty-four of chronic nephritis. In 1926, John sold his bar holdings and built a comfortable home in Lewiston Orchards where he enjoyed a serene life. When Philip and his parents moved in with his grandfather in 1934, he remembered his grandfather's home to be a warm and welcoming refuge.

"We got along well, but we didn't have to stay long with granddad because my father got a state job and we moved," said Philip.

When John celebrated his ninety-ninth birthday, a newspaper reporter asked him if he had a recipe for a long life. Philip's grandfather summed it up in two words—hard work. He went on to say, "I tell my sons and all other young men, they don't know what hard work is. I worked for a dollar a day when I was a boy and worked hard."

Philip said, "A lifetime that spans a century is more than the number of years allowed to most men, but my grandfather lived to be one hundred years of age." He remained cheerful and laughed frequently. On January 20, 1948, John Edward Bishop died. He was survived by his three sons—Philip Edward, John Alfred, Charles Fields, and his two daughters, Margaret Harrington and Clarissa Frances Norris.

CHAPTER 5

The Young Adult

✦✦✦✦

In 1934, at age sixteen, 110 pounds and about 5'2" tall, Philip graduated from Lewiston High School. He hadn't been a wonderful student and, because he lived eight miles away, he rode the school bus and wasn't able to participate in school activities. Driving a car in those days was only used for necessities.

After Philip had tried his hand at farm work, he went to work for a taxidermy fur shop in Lewiston. He had taken a correspondence course in taxidermy and took a job in a shop where there was an excellent teacher. The teacher was the owner of the shop and had Philip do all the dirty work such as fleshing hides, cleaning coats, and other mundane duties. He worked ten hours a day, six days a week, and was paid thirteen dollars per week.

Philip worked in the basement of the shop. Coats were made upstairs where five women, including the owner's wife, prepared the expensive furs. "One day I had a question, and on impulse, I ran up the stairs to see the boss. I wore tennis shoes, so he didn't hear me coming. I saw him all right. I stood there with my mouth open. The owner was standing near the top of the stairs kissing and clutching one of his seamstresses, and it wasn't his wife! His wife was fifteen feet away working behind a curtained area. When they saw me, they untangled themselves. The lady was very embarrassed, but it didn't bother him. In fact, a day later he asked if I wanted to go fishing! Neither my boss nor I ever mentioned the incident again. His wife, and her sister who lived with them, always seemed sad and unhappy. I think a lot went on that I didn't know about. I worked for him about a year before I got a job at a local saw mill."

Philip learned that persistence paid off when he finally landed the sawmill job. While he was still working at the taxidermy shop, he begged his neighbor, a foreman in the Lewiston sawmill, for a job. The neighbor insisted Philip was too small to handle the heavy work in his section. Philip didn't give up asking for a job, and when he turned eighteen and had grown a little more (he eventually grew to be 5'8" tall), the neighbor hired him to work in a section called the *four squares* department. The men in that department packaged the very best number one grade lumber, and shipped the majority of the lumber to the East coast. His wages were forty cents an hour, which added up to three dollars and twenty cents for an eight-hour day. This was considered a fabulous wage, so everyone in town wanted a job at the sawmill. The neighbor was sure Philip would be fired in short order, but Philip held his own among several large men. One fellow in particular who was in charge, did his best to get Philip to quit by showing him the difficult way of doing the work. This treatment continued for several weeks. Philip was tenacious and not about to give in. The fellow finally realized Philip wasn't going to quit and began showing him the easier way of doing things. He worked at the mill for two years until he decided he wasn't going to work in a sawmill for the rest of his life. He quit and went to business college in Boise.

During Philip's sawmill days, he purchased a 1934 Ford V-8 Coupe. "It ran like a rabbit, and in fact, I was arrested for speeding twice. I just barely missed going to jail in Colfax,

Washington. Several of us were going to Spokane for a wild weekend. On the way, we were priming ourselves with some beer. On a long straight stretch of road, I decided to see just how fast my car was. At about sixty-five miles per hour, we passed an old car and one of my buddies stuck his head out and yelled 'get out and crank it.' It turned out it was a deputy sheriff and he did crank it. He took us back to Colfax and stood us immediately before the judge. The judge ruled that I needed to pay twenty-five dollars or spend twenty-five days in jail. We pooled our money. Broke and wiser, we ended our splendid weekend."

After his Ford, Philip purchased an Indian Chief motorcycle at a cost of seventy-five dollars. He rode it to work, and later from Lewiston to Boise. It was a heavy machine weighing three hundred pounds and had no crash guards. If the motorcycle went down, it was imperative to keep one's legs out from under the machine. He crashed it several times, but always managed to stay on the topside. One time he dislocated his hip and wound up in a chiropractor's office. He attended college in Moscow, Idaho, at the time, and on one Sunday as he drove from Lewiston to Moscow, he failed to make a turn. He and his bike went down into a small canyon. He was thrown off, and in the process, dislocated his hip again. He was able to get the bike back on the road and make his way to town. Back to the chiropractor.

Philip was always looking for ways to earn money. Idahoans and Americans across the nation were still living in the grip of the Depression. When he learned there was an Idaho National Guard Cavalry mounted unit in Lewiston, he enlisted as a Private First Class in September, 1936.

The unit was formed in 1929, and consisted of about sixty-five men during the 1920s and 1930s. The cavalry's mission was to maintain current standards of military discipline as well as to preserve the specialized skills and traditions of the horse-mounted cavalry of a bygone era.

The use of horses in warfare began over 5,000 years ago. The first United States designated cavalry was authorized by Congress in 1855. During the Civil War (1861-1865), the cavalry proved to be the most important and respected role in the American military. The cavalry continued to be used extensively during the nineteenth century; however, by the beginning of the twentieth century, horses became less important for use in warfare. Light cavalry was still used on the battlefield at the beginning of the twentieth century, but it began to be phased out for combat during and soon after World War I. Immediately prior to World War II, the United States Cavalry transitioned to a mechanized force. Horses were replaced by tanks, armored vehicles, helicopters for transportation, and aircraft for reconnaissance. Still, some cavalry units did have military uses well into World War II.

During World War II, the 26th Cavalry was the only American cavalry to be used. This valiant cavalry was a formidable force against the Japanese invaders of Luzon. They held valuable ground while the Allied armies retreated to Bataan.

While Philip was in training in the Cavalry in Lewiston, he witnessed a tragic accident with one of the horses. There was an exercise that involved riding at a gallop on a circular course and shooting silhouette targets. The cavalrymen in his unit were armed with .45 caliber semi-automatic pistols.

"You held your reins in your left hand and your pistol in your right," said Philip. " A fellow soldier mishandled his pistol and accidentally shot his horse in the head. I can still hear the company commander screaming."

Philip said his horse was extremely temperamental. "He was

the nastiest horse in the whole damn company. Nobody wanted to ride him. He would bite you, kick you and he would shake his head until it got low enough to try to buck you off."

Philip spent two years in the horse cavalry and was discharged in September of 1938. Finally, by 1940, the days of the cavalry unit came to end in Lewiston, Idaho.

In 1939, Philip rode his motorcycle to Boise where he took a job flipping a few hamburgers in a pool hall and also went to business college. He took general business courses including shorthand and typing. Philip paid for most of his tuition by cleaning the school building on Saturdays and after school.

On September 1, 1939, the day Hitler invaded Poland to begin World War II, Philip was attending business school and partying. "I was so consumed with my own life that one of the most momentous events in all history, Hitler's *blitzkrieg*, barely got my attention. Little did I know that event would change my life."

CHAPTER 6

Just One Year of Duty

◆◆◆

On September 16, 1940, twenty-three-year-old Philip Bishop jumped into the back of a two-and-a-half-ton truck and was on his way to Fort Lewis, Washington, for one year of military training in the National Guard. Since he had previously served in the Horse Cavalry in Lewiston, Idaho, he had some limited military training. Philip's father learned the Idaho National Guard was being mobilized for one year of training at Fort Lewis and set up a meeting with the company commander of the 116th Engineer Battalion Headquarters and Service Company to talk about his son. When the company commander learned Philip was a business college student, he knew Philip was the perfect candidate to recruit. The commander was desperate to have someone who could type and take shorthand. The commander informed Philip that if he enlisted, he would immediately promote him from a private to a sergeant. Philip thought, *How hard could it be? I'll put in my year and be done with it.* "Son, get your year in and get it over with," his dad said. Philip enlisted as a buck private in the rear rank and had no ambitions to become anything else.

"I went with the Guard, I thought, for one year. It was supposed to fulfill my military obligation and then I would be, once again, a civilian and proceed with making my *fortune.* This didn't work out."

When he arrived at Fort Lewis, he and the other recruits were placed in a camp called Mud (Camp) Murray located three or four miles south of Fort Lewis proper. The camp consisted of tents with each tent accommodating six men. The camp received its nickname, Mud Murray, because of the frequent rainfall resulting in mud everywhere about six inches deep. They had to walk on boardwalks.

"We ate c-rations. It was canned food. It was like dog food in a can. They heated up a tub of water and put the cans of food into the hot water to heat them up. As the soldiers came by, they handed us a can and a can opener. Half of the time, when I opened it up, it squirted out onto my shirt front. And it stunk. It was the most terrible tasting stuff that I had ever eaten."

Philip was assigned to Battalion Headquarters of the 116th Engineer Battalion, 41st Infantry Division, where he worked using his typing and shorthand skills for the adjutant, who was a captain from Boise. "He seemed to think I was fine and dandy and he said very soon he would see that I became a sergeant, but there was a problem I didn't understand at that time." The adjutant failed to inform Philip about the Table of Organization that dictated the number of privates, corporals and sergeants allowed in a company. Philip learned the Battalion was already over a couple of sergeants. He became the leading enlisted soldier, but he was still a private. At least he was his adjutant's pet who kept him out of mundane duty like KP. He insisted that Philip should be at headquarters at all times.

Philip began to consume alcohol. It never occurred to him that drinking was hazardous to his health. Everybody drank. After about six months, the adjutant told him a staff sergeant was getting a commission and Philip would be getting the sergeant's stripes. Philip thought he should celebrate and went to nearby Tacoma. He got drunk and failed to return to camp. Philip Bishop was AWOL. Back at camp, his tent mates covered for him and said Philip had gone to headquarters early. At headquarters, someone said he was sick. Back in Tacoma, Philip decided to call the First Sergeant and tell him he would be back soon. Not knowing about the cover-ups on his behalf in camp, this proved to be a poor decision. When he reported to the Company Commander, he was reprimanded with seven days of KP and told Philip he was to serve it out on weekends.

"I knew that a seven-day restriction had to be consecutively served, so I intended to do my first weekend, and then produce the Army regulation. Somebody got wise, and the next morning at 4:00 a.m., I was awakened for KP duty. Additionally, the adjutant said I had screwed up my promotion for a good six months. A couple of months later, I was promoted to Staff Sergeant."

"I really didn't give a damn until Sunday morning on December 7, 1941, when I awoke to find the Japs had attacked Pearl Harbor, and the gates to leave camp were locked. Everyone was numb with shock, saddened, and furious about the sneak attack. It dawned on me I was about to become a professional soldier. This changed my entire outlook. I hadn't been trying to progress up the soldier's ladder at all. I was just letting things ride as they were. So, I decided I should become an officer.

"First, I decided to become a hot fighter pilot, so I went to McChord Field for my physical and mental tests. I took all sorts of written tests for knowledge and psychomotor tests for manual dexterity. I felt sure of myself. Nothing in any of those tests was beyond my capabilities. Then came the test for color blindness. It became clear I was color blind as a bat. No hope for the Air Force which used all types of color signals."

During that time, the Battalion used IQ tests. As it turned out, Philip's IQ was higher than most, including the officers. It was suggested he should apply for Officer Candidate School, also known as the *school for ninety-day wonders*. Philip liked this idea and applied, and after four months, was accepted.

Philip said he was nearly not accepted due to his color blindness, and had to have a special dispensation. "They sent me to an old doctor. The doctor said, 'How bad do you want to go to Officer's Candidate School?' I answered that I really wanted to go. Then the doctor said, 'Okay, what is the color of that object in that picture up there on the wall?' It was a picture of a fire engine. So I answered, 'it's red.' He said, 'That's very good.' The doctor called my color blindness not *disqualifying*."

Soon, Philip was at Fort Belvoir, Virginia, where he was double-timed and endured ninety days of hell. There were constant inspections of barracks, latrines, bunks, weapons, footlockers, clothing and personal appearance.

Philip described the inspections. "There were many full barrack inspections. All lockers had to be opened and be in neat array. The bed with the olive drab blanket had to be taught and springy. If there was a speck of dirt, or a coin when dropped that didn't bounce off the bed's blanket, or if there was an untidy bunk area, you went on latrine and garbage details and were restricted to quarters. In the field, there were inspections wherein the soldiers had to line up outside their tents displaying all of their equipment and to be standing at attention. There were inspections while we were in platoon formation, for neatness of dress, shoes shined, clean-shaven and spotless guns. In the inspection of guns, the officer, wearing white gloves, would inspect every gun as each soldier was in the position of *port arms*. He would snap the rifle, look down the barrel and hand the rifle back to the soldier. A lieutenant, inspecting the platoon, faced me while I was at port arms. Seeing the small movement of his eyes, before he made a grab for my rifle, I let go. The rifle fell to the ground as he made a grab for the inspection. I didn't flinch nor move and stayed at attention. After an awkward moment, he stooped and picked up my rifle and handed it back to me with a smirk on his face and continued his inspection. Soldiers were to let go of their rifle as soon as the officer motioned to inspect it. This day, he was a fraction too slow.

"This was in basic training. The tactical officer tried hard to flunk us for very minor problems. Demerits were issued right and left. So many demerits required walking a phony guard post on Saturday and Sundays. One week I was standing for Saturday inspection without a single demerit. It appeared I was about to have a weekend in Washington, D.C. The inspection began. I snapped my rifle up for the first inspection. He barely glanced at it and said, 'Rusty rifle.' I had just received ten demerits and there was no chance my rifle was rusty. Getting no response from me, the tactical officer pulled out my bayonet. Again, he said 'Rusty bayonet.' Another ten demerits. My weekend was determined, but it wouldn't be in Washington. This type of treatment was followed by the question, 'Do you agree with me, Mr.?' Any answer other than 'Yes sir,' Officer Candidate School was over.

"We had map and compass readings, lectures, nomenclatures and taking apart and assembling all types of weapons, and can you believe listening to the *Articles of War* again? We had machine gun training and pistol firing. The non-coms taught us how to hold, aim and squeeze the trigger. 'Squeeze it like a lemon,' they would shout. At first most of the men were jerking and pulling on the trigger causing them to miss the targets. They weren't teaching me anything new, I had been shooting since I was seven years old. We were also taught how to lay a minefield with the idea that at some future time, the mine field would have to be cleared. We used compasses to get coordinates and make a grid plot plan and set the mines in a pattern so that they could be located.

"The close order drills were orders such as columns, right or left, to the rear march, oblique right or left, forward march, first squad to the right, left or rear march, etc. And about-face, right or left face. In my early days, this was no problem as I was always in the middle of the platoon marching and trying to stay in step. Later on, because of my size, I was put on the right front (lead). Then it was very funny. I was bawled out by the sergeant as he barked 'Column right.' I didn't know how to turn or move and stumbled and screwed up the whole platoon. No one ever showed me or taught me how. I learned quickly to pivot after that incident. In time, I considered myself a very good drill sergeant in Manual of Arms, drills and posting of guards and becoming a first-class soldier.

"During the last month, we went through a three-day exercise. It started on a Thursday and went straight through to Saturday inspection. After inspection, the company commander said, 'Anyone deserving a pass may have one.' I staggered up to his office, picked up my pass and went to Washington. I got a hotel room and decided to have a short nap before checking out the town. My nap lasted until Sunday noon, and I was due to walk a tour on Sunday at 2:00 p.m. I went back to camp, grabbed my rifle and hit the drill field. Another fun weekend. Every time there was a cut, which was frequent, I figured I was gone. But ninety days later, I put on my little gold bars, a full-fledged ninety-day wonder as a dashing Second Lieutenant."

Philip was assigned to the 10th Corps Engineer Battalion as a platoon leader and was shipped to Camp Carson, Colorado. After six months of harassment by an old eccentric colonel who had thirty-five years of service under his belt, Philip was given a platoon of men straight out of civilian life from New York City. When he met the train, and saw the group of derelict looking men he was to train, he seriously thought about trying to retire on the spot. They were in civilian clothes and looked like hoodlums or mob members. The entire group was white since in those days blacks and whites were separated, and usually, there were no black combat units. This group of men didn't know the first thing about marching and saluting, and it was up to Philip to make good soldiers out of them. A year later, Philip was proud of these men whom he transformed into genuine soldiers.

In 1943, Philip's Battalion went to Camp Polk, Louisiana. In September near the end of the maneuvers, there was a request from the War Department for the Battalion to furnish four combat platoon commanders for immediate shipment overseas. Four unmarried commanders were chosen, and Philip was one of them. They anticipated heavy engineer casualties in Africa, and the four officers were to replace combat engineer officers lost. Philip said he hated leaving his unit, but was eager to enter into combat. Later, he would realize this was one of the dumbest things he had ever thought of.

On their way toward the distant shores of battle, they traveled by rail across the nation. The Union Pacific Railroad's main rail line ran through the isolated plains town of North Platte, Nebraska. Day and night the troop trains, filled with young men being transported across America destined to be shipped out, rolled into North Platte.

North Platte was special to all these young men. When the war broke out, a local resident came up with an idea. *Why don't the residents meet the trains filled with the soldiers coming through town, and offer them affection, gratitude, and support?* The plan came to fruition on Christmas Day, 1941. When the train rolled into the depot, the unsuspecting soldiers were greeted with welcoming words, heartfelt smiles, and baskets of food. The residents and businesses donated everything. What started out as an idea turned into something amazing. Before long, the depot transformed into a lunch counter at the Union Pacific Railroad station and became known as the North Platte Canteen. The Canteen provided food, coffee and milk, cigarettes, and magazines. The volunteers offered the soldiers anything they wanted such as sandwiches, deviled eggs, homemade pickles, cookies, doughnuts, and cake. One lady would grind roast beef with a hand grinder for beef salad sandwiches. It was open every day from 5:00 a.m. until the last troop train passed through after midnight. On each day during the war, an estimated 3,000 to 5,000 military personnel came through North Platte. The trains were scheduled to stop for only ten minutes, but the generous people of North Platte made every minute count. More than 125 communities around North Platte made sure the Canteen was fully staffed. Even with gasoline being so limited, one way or another, the people found a way to get to the depot. They dropped what they were doing to participate.

Men, women, and children volunteering their time greeted the soldiers. It was their way of saying *thank you*. The townspeople looked into the faces of so many young men—some were teenagers. Most of these soldiers had never been away from home, and now they were heading into the unknown. Some would not return. The people knew it, and offered warmth and love in that small snapshot of time.

Philip recalled his own experience. "I remember the tasty food and coffee. But that wasn't the biggest thing about it. Those people made you feel really appreciated. Those happy smiles you saw. I know it sounds like a simple thing. But I was heading for an infantry division, and I didn't know where I would end up. And I never forgot those smiles. You have no idea what it meant to us. We came through in the middle of the night, and they were there."

On their way to the port of embarkation, the soldiers went through several replacement depots where they would stay for several days before proceeding on to the next stop. When they arrived in Shenango, Pennsylvania, they would be on a ten-day stay. Philip and one of his friends wanted some excitement, so they decided to go to Youngstown, Ohio. Youngstown was a bigger town and offered better possibilities to find some action. They were going to go by bus, but the line at the bus station was so long, they decided to hitchhike.

"The first evening, two lovely ladies picked us up who had whiskey, cigarettes, and plenty of time. So, the next evening, my friend and I decided hitch hiking was our ticket. Soon a car with two ladies went past. They studied us, but didn't stop until they were about four hundred yards down the road. This time we were stuck in the back seat with the two ladies in the front. Both ladies were nicely dressed in wool suits and well-polished pumps. Both wore shoulder-length brunette hair in curls. And both were good looking. Suggestions that we pair up didn't work too well and they dumped us out in Youngstown. They were off to see their grandmother, they said.

"Several hours later, whom should we meet, but the same two ladies. One of them was Valerie Stefanowicz. She said it was a coincidence, but I say they were looking for us. Anyhow, we all went out together, and every night from that night on, Valerie and I went out. After about seven or eight days, I was shipped to a port of embarkation in New Jersey. We talked on the telephone daily. I had been around dozens of women in my past, but *she was different*. I realized I was in love. I knew I had to do something and do it soon— *Valerie may not wait for me to return home*. The less time I had, the harder it became to do anything. I was almost panic-stricken. Then finally on the phone, I blurted out, 'How would you like to get married?' With only a couple days before I left for Europe, she could refuse me, and I would have only a short time to feel embarrassed. But she had been waiting for this question, so she gave me an immediate 'Yes!'

"Valerie had some relatives in Jersey City, and one worked for the city. He manipulated a fast marriage license and waived the obligatory blood test, and on September 26, 1943, on a Sunday, we were married. I still remember several of her aunts who weren't at all sure that Valerie was doing a smart thing by marrying a second lieutenant who was due to ship out on Monday, the next day. Getting married after a two-week relationship was probably the most spontaneous and risky thing either of us had done up to that point in our lives. One day later, I boarded a ship for England. Valerie went back to her job in Shenango where she worked for the Engineering Department. I wrote a lot of letters and she wrote almost every day. Some honeymoon!"

Volunteers greeting soldiers at the North Platte Canteen in North Platte, Nebraska, 1941-1946. (Picture courtesy of the Lincoln County Historical Society, North Platte, Nebraska)

Philip & Valerie, married September 26, 1943

CHAPTER 7

Away and At Home

◆◆◆◆

On Monday, the day after their wedding, Philip was on his way to Europe for two years, and his bride was on her way home to wait for him. While Philip would be living the war, Valerie would be dealing with the stress of wondering if she would ever see her husband alive again. Valerie and millions of Americans on the home front hovered around their radio daily to hear any sliver of news about what was happening over there. They could only hope there wouldn't be a knock on their door with a delivery of the dreaded Western Union telegram with news that their loved one wasn't coming home.

Mail from overseas was the highlight for those waiting to hear the latest news from their warrior. The soldiers wrote as often as they could. In fact, because there were so many letters written overseas, the letters couldn't be shipped to the home front. So, the Armed Forces came up with the solution of putting the letters on microfilm, which was then shipped to the United States to be reprinted stateside. This type of mail was called V-Mail. Valerie checked her mailbox every day for a letter from Philip. He tried to write daily, but sometimes several days would go by without any sign of a letter from him causing Valerie a great deal of worry. Sometimes two or three letters would arrive at one time. The writers had to be discreet with their words. The letters were censored to make sure there wasn't any sensitive information about the war.

Philip's home state of Idaho played an important role in the war. There were approximately sixty thousand Idahoans who served—1,784 of them died, eight were missing in action, and thirty became prisoners of war.

Bountiful Idaho became a key state for providing food which included beef, mutton, pork, turkey, chicken, eggs, potatoes, beans, peas, onions, sweet corn, apples, prunes, peaches, cherries, milk, cheese, and butter.

Lumber became an important contribution to the war effort. The Idaho mills at Potlatch, Coeur d'Alene, and Philip's hometown of Lewiston, produced four hundred twenty-seven million board feet of lumber consisting of white pine and yellow (ponderosa) pine.

Idaho provided minerals. Her lead was used to make bullets and batteries, zinc was used in making brass cartridges, and mercury exploded the percussion caps. Silver was used to make silver alloy bearings, and tungsten was used in making hard-cutting tools in war plants.

Just as they did in World War I, women in Idaho and across the nation joined the labor forces to replace the men who were no longer there, and those women who stayed home planted *victory gardens* which supplied forty percent of the vegetables consumed on the home front. They utilized every piece of land that was suitable for planting a garden. Women volunteered to help salvage war materials and helped to sell war bonds. They organized scrap drives for steel, tin, paper and rubber. Since nylon was needed for the war effort, women could no longer buy hose. Instead, they painted their legs with a lotion that came in the shades of the stockings and even drew the dark seam line down the back of their legs. Bare legs were patriotic.

Many Idahoans switched from agricultural labor and worked in shipyards, airplane assembly plants, and aluminum reduction plants. This change caused a shortage in the agricultural labor force resulting in the Idaho farmers recruiting help through the Mexican *bracero* program. It wasn't long before farmers tapped into other labor resources. They were able to strengthen their labor forces from the Japanese-Americans who had been relocated to Idaho, the prisoner of war camps, and even the Navajo Indians who lived on reservations in southern Utah, Arizona, and New Mexico.

During this time, the people of Idaho watched their population grow in unexpected ways. In the period of September 1942 through October 1945, because of panicked distrust of the Japanese, approximately ten thousand Japanese-Americans were yanked from their homes in Seattle and Portland to be relocated to a desert location in south central Idaho on the Snake River plain. Their new home, Minidoka Center at Hunt, consisted of row after row of low black barracks of frame and tarpaper. This group formed the eighth largest city in Idaho at that time.

Idaho also became the home for many German and Italian prisoners of war. The camps were set up in several towns and strategically located near the farms and orchards where labor was desperately needed. The farmers paid them the required minimum wage of two dollars and twenty cents per day. The prisoners lived in tents surrounded by hog wire fences. Early each morning, the guards transported the prisoners to the work fields. One German prison soldier commented, "Hitler proclaimed we would march across North America. Instead, here I am on American soil on my hands and knees."

The United States dutifully followed the Geneva Convention rules. The prisoners' food was equal to that of the American soldier, and they received excellent medical care at the base hospitals. The prisoners were allowed to organize sports activities, enjoy motion pictures, musical instruments, crafts, libraries, and camp newspapers. Many of the prisoners took courses in American history and the English language. Life in an American prisoner of war camp was a luxury compared to the cruel treatment Americans received in the German and Japanese prisoner of war camps.

Idaho experienced a surging prosperous economy, and with the mix of the Hispanic *braceros*, the relocated Japanese-Americans, and the prisoners of war who stayed after the war, the state evolved into a diverse ethnic populace.

CHAPTER 8

Off To War

❖❖❖

Philip thought he was going into combat in Africa. He and the other combat engineers were intended to be the replacement for the almost certain loss of combat engineers in Africa. Instead, their transport ship zigzagged for ten days across the Atlantic to England. The anticipated losses in Africa didn't occur. Philip recalled, "I found myself in the ship's hold among the throng of GI's. Bunks were stacked four-high. The stink of seasick vomit, thousand-man body odor, thick smell of diesel fuel and the constant rolling of the ship was almost more than I could take." They thought they had one close call near England when a German plane flew over the ship. The ship changed direction to slip into a huge fog bank for cover. The final leg of the journey went without incident.

When they disembarked in England, they were assigned to a non-combatant unit. Philip was anxious to get into the fight and immediately tried to transfer out of the assigned unit.

"We were all in England with very little to do. And most of us were pretty unhappy about this situation because we didn't have any unit we could go into. It was hell, and I drank a lot," Philip said. Then he tried to get into the Airborne as a paratrooper, but was unsuccessful. "This probably saved my neck because a good number of the paratroopers were killed when they went over across in the D-Day invasion."

Then he was assigned to be a glider pilot. At the time, there weren't enough gliders available for the recruits, so Philip was told to stay in his unit until more gliders came in. Glider pilots were initially recruited from Army pilots, but as the demand increased for pilots, they recruited enlisted soldiers with no flight experience. The glider was a framework of steel tubing and a painted canvas skin with a plywood floor and seats. It was engineless with only the prevailing winds to power it to a safe landing, and the only gauge provided was one to determine the elevation. It was unarmed, and there were no parachutes. Provisions were limited. The purpose of the glider was to transport troops or to deliver supplies to troops isolated on the front lines. The glider was towed up into the air to 1,000 feet by a tow airplane to the destination, and once detached from the airplane, quietly glided down to the drop zone. If they were shot at, they had no defense. Landings were dangerous with many possible obstructions such as trees, hedgerows or buildings, and landing under cover of darkness was even more dangerous. The flight was a one-way ticket. Once on the ground, the pilot had to either enter an ongoing battle in the locale or find a way back to safety with his limited provisions.

Philip was ready and waiting to take on the challenge, but there were still no gliders available. Then the invasion began, and he was removed from the glider pilot list. He was certain that probably saved his life. The glider pilot casualties were exceedingly high.

Philip sat around England for several more months until finally he received orders to transfer to France. While he was waiting for his assignment to a unit, he was put in charge of a platoon of trucks in an operation called the Red Ball Express. There was a need, and the Red Ball Express Highway was born to meet that need. It began in August of 1944. Many of the trucks wore red ball symbols on the front bumpers. Designated road signs marked the highway showing large red balls centered on white placards to designate the Red Ball Highway. Engineers also created one-way signs and signs warning unauthorized military vehicles or French drivers to stay off the highway. Speed was of the utmost importance. Anyone who saw a Red Ball truck barreling down the road knew to get out of the way immediately.

Following is information and excellent detail about the Red Ball Express gleaned from the article contributed by Kelly Heathman, Historian and Equipment Analyst 2 in Northwest Region, May 9, 2002, WSDOT, Traffic & Roads:

Of the many unsung heroes of the Second World War were the men of the US Army Transportation Corps, Motor Transport Service. Although these young men were not on the front lines, they proved to the world the vital importance of a well-regulated transportation system, in the struggle to defeat the Nazis during the Second World War.

A shining example of their contributions is the story of the truck drivers and highway system of the Red Ball Express.

During the invasion of France in June of 1944, the Allied Armies struggled to advance across Europe. The retreating German armies destroyed the French railroads which meant that the advancing Allied Armies had to be supplied by truck.

While General Patton's Third Army made great strides, the army needed immediate re-supply of fuel for the tanks and combat vehicles at the front. "My men can eat their belts," Patton was overhead telling Eisenhower, "but my tanks gotta have gas." World War II was truly a mechanized war, or as one observer noted a "one-hundred-percent-combustion engine war." The advance was in jeopardy of grinding to a halt.

The Red Ball was born to provide 750 tons of supplies a day that each of the twenty-eight divisions advancing across France and Belgium required. The name came from a railroad term to red ball or ship something express. Trucks and drivers were in short supply in the Motor Transport Service in Europe, so the army raided any units that had any to spare in a desperate effort to bridge the gap between the supplies back in Normandy and the armies at the front. Many of the drivers given the task of supplying the front with precious fuel were from non-combat units.

The first Red Ball convoys quickly jammed up in military and civilian traffic. In response, the Transportation Corps devised a two-lane 'loop run' highway system expressly for the use of the Red Ball. No other military or civilian traffic was allowed. The route ran from the supply depots near Normandy to just south of Paris, approximately a six-hundred-mile-round trip. The Transportation Corps Engineers maintained the roads and bridges along the highway system. The roads were in constant need of repair not only because of the relentless beating of the trucks, but also because of enemy aircraft and mines. Truckers would place sandbags on the floorboards of the trucks to protect themselves from the blast of mines. They were also in danger of being strafed by enemy aircraft, so some of the trucks had ring-mounted 0.30 or 0.50 caliber machine guns on the top of the cab for anti-aircraft action.

Signs and markers were placed along the route, and Military Police were on hand at major checkpoints to direct traffic. Disabled vehicles were moved to the side of the road where they were either repaired by Ordinance units or sent back to the rear area repair shops.

The round trip took approximately fifty-four hours to complete in the two and one-half ton truck known as a deuce and a half. These trucks took a tremendous beating. Tire replacement alone doubled to over 50,000 in the month of September. The trucks ran around the clock, and the drivers were supposed to follow a strict set of rules. Vehicles could not exceed thirty-five miles per hour; no passing was allowed; each convoy was to have five trucks with a lead and follow jeep. However, because the front was moving so rapidly, the actual movement was described as a 'free-for-all at a stock car race.'

Drivers were pushed to the limit and lack of sleep was a problem. Men would fall asleep, slump over, bump into the truck in front of them, and then wake back up. The Red Ball Express lasted just three months from late August to mid November, 1944. The truck and highway system known as the Red Ball Express had completed its mission. The system moved fuel to the front quickly and bought precious time to the rear-echelon support teams to build up the railroads and pipelines needed to supply the Allied Armies into Germany.

Colonel John S.D. Eisenhower wrote: "The spectacular nature of the advance was due in as great a measure to the men who drove the Red Ball trucks as to those who drove the tanks. Without it, the advance could never have been made."

Philip and his men quartered in a tent camp west of Paris. His job was to take twenty empty trucks from outside of Paris to Cherbourg Post, pick up supplies of all types, and deliver them to units on the line. All they carried for themselves were K-rations, drinking water and gasoline for the trucks. They slept whenever they could get a chance which was mainly in their trucks. They met many obstacles along the way, such as strafing by the Luftwaffe, mined roads or German spies and sympathizers. They added guards on to their trucks when they learned there were some French hooligans waiting on steep hills ready to jump onto the back of the slower trucks to snatch and throw off some of the supplies.

Philip recalled a moment with General Patton. "I decided I wanted to be the driver of our truck, but I was a little slow. Then, I became aware of a car behind me with the driver beeping his horn at me. I looked in the rear view mirror, and there was Patton standing up with his fist in the air. I figured I'd better speed up."

There is a quote from General Patton that seems most appropriate: *Lead me, follow me, or get out of my way.*

After three or four trips, Philip received his new assignment.

CHAPTER 9

Ready For Combat

◆◆◆

Next, Philip was assigned to be a platoon leader of the Ninth Armored Division. The division had just fought a brutal battle at Bastogne and suffered heavy losses. The battle proved to be the most difficult and trying period of the division's history. Philip replaced one of the soldiers killed during the battle, and he was anxious to join the fight. On December 28, 1944, he left Paris in an unheated railroad car to go to Metz, France. The railroad car, called a forty and eight, meant that it held forty men or eight horses. There were no seats—just a boxcar, and it was cold. One time they found some creosote railroad ties and burned them in the boxcar for heat. They didn't realize the black-creosoted smoke would cause lung problems. At one stop where they would be fed, Philip jumped out of the railroad car and ran through the snow toward the chow line that had been set up for their train convoy. "I ran about fifty yards and went down in a dead faint when the cold air hit my creosoted lungs. It didn't stop me. I got back up and hit the chow line."

After the men finished eating, they loaded back onto the train. At about two o'clock in the morning, the train arrived at the *get-off* point. It was extremely cold weather with a foot of snow and freezing wind. They walked through the snow for four or five miles to their billet in what was left of a German village. Philip recalled, "There wasn't a single building left with a roof." The soldiers, exhausted from wading through the snowdrifts, bedded down in a bombed-out shelter until morning.

"From my cold little home, I could see flashes from the German 88s firing on the line units. I was green. Fresh from commanding a trucking company on the Red Ball Express, I had no idea of what to do in this new situation. I was astounded at the seemingly casual attitude of the other soldiers toward the enemy. But I soon learned being casual in the face of the enemy was only a front which combat soldiers sometimes used to hide their feelings."

Several days later, Philip caught up with his new unit where he was assigned as a platoon leader of Company C, Ninth Armored Engineers. He realized being a good platoon leader was a lonely job. He said, "I didn't want to really get to know anybody over there because it was bad enough to lose a man—I was damned sure I didn't want to lose a friend. But as hard as I tried not to get involved with my men, I still couldn't help liking them and getting close."

Because there were no barracks in France, the troops stayed in the French villages in houses, warehouses or hotels. Philip billeted for several weeks in a house with an old French couple. "It was colder than a well digger's butt in the mornings. Every morning at 6 a.m., the old man came into my room and burned a few twigs hoping to heat the house a degree or two," Philip said.

During the day, the troops trained in the snow and participated in classes, calisthenics, and lectures. Anything to keep the men busy.

The combat engineers trained and became experts in mines and explosives. One of Philip's first duties was to refresh the troops on German mines. To do this, he gathered real mines out of nearby fields. The troops didn't know Philip well yet, so they stepped back while he dismantled the mines. Philip didn't experience any close calls dismantling the mines, but a commander of the Ninth Armored Division lost fifteen to twenty men when a soldier made the mistake of handling a German mine while sitting on a large pile of recovered mines.

Philip described life in the Armored Division:

"The Allies formed armored divisions after observing the success of the German *blitzkrieg* tactics at the beginning of the war using tanks and armored infantry units. The Ninth was activated at Fort Riley, Kansas, in July of 1942, and after the soldiers in the division completed intensive military training in both California and Louisiana, the Ninth Armored Division arrived in England in August of 1944. An armored infantry battalion consists of four platoons of rifle, machine gun and motor squads. There are also service and headquarter companies consisting of eleven hundred enlisted men and forty officers. The officers for each battalion include the commanding officer, executive officer, company commanders, and company platoon lieutenants. I was a company platoon lieutenant. An armored division has about 14,000 men. I was armed with a 30-cal., sixteen-shot carbine in charge of fifty-five men and five half-tracks. The men were armed with M-1 Garand rifles. Most officers not armed with carbines usually carried side arms (Colt 45s).

"Many officers used Jeeps (Willys) leading convoys, carrying supplies, and when necessary, evacuating a wounded soldier or transporting a prisoner back to the command post for interrogation. Our half-tracks had two front wheels and two treaded rear tank tracks. They were armed with a 50-cal. gun behind the driver and the half-track commander. The half-track carried a squad of twelve men consisting of a driver, the commander, and ten armed infantry soldiers. The half-track weighed approximately ten tons of heavy tank-like steel. They carried water and gas in G.I. cans. There were rails on the outside of the vehicle holding unfused mines. Some half-tracks would tow a 37mm or 57mm canon. The 37mm gun was useless and the 57mm wasn't much better. A half-track's speed could accelerate up to approximately forty-five miles per hour with a range of one hundred miles. With their speed, the half-tracks could quickly move troops to help clear obstacles for their tanks. When going on an attack and dismounting from the half-track, we would take only what we needed for combat to our objective. All other equipment was left behind in the half-track.

"A combat soldier had bandoliers of 30-cal. ammunition, a rifle belt with cartridges, two grenades hanging on his belt, a canteen and his weapon and bayonet. If he had to be away from the half-track for any length of time, then he would take his full field equipment of clothing, mess kit with fork, knife and spoon, small shovel and pick for digging foxholes, some c-rations and toiletries. It was no fun, but the job had to be done.

"The foxholes were slit trenches dug by the soldiers to protect themselves from enemy fire and strafing planes. Even when the rains half-filled the foxholes, we still jumped into them for protection from the enemy and the Luftwaffe. Most of the Luftwaffe was destroyed near the end of the war. Many were shot down in dogfights, and planes on the ground were bombed and strafed. These planes weren't airborne because of the lack of fuel. What a beautiful sight to see a dogfight and an enemy plane crashing to the ground. Just one less plane to strafe our troops!

"The well-equipped soldier would go into combat dressed in olive drab (O.D.) clothes, combat suit, combat boots, fatigues and rain gear. A blouse, an olive-drab-colored jacket, was worn on dress occasions which was later replaced by a real snazzy Eisenhower jacket. In summertime, we dressed in suntans.

"Our tanks were light, medium and heavy, manned by a crew of five. The M-3 light tank (Lee & Stuart) had two and one-half inch armor plate, a six-man crew, with fire power of a 75mm gun,

37mm turret gun and three 30-cal. machine guns. They were effective in giving support to ground troops against enemy infantry, but were like tin cans and no match for the German Tiger and Panther tanks, manned by a crew of six. The difference between a tanker soldier and an infantry soldier was the tanker provided a steel barrier to protect him, while an infantry soldier had only his shirt to stop a bullet. The medium-sized tanks were better, had a greater range, and were mobile. Our best model, the Sherman, held its own in close proximity to enemy tanks and was more of a match for the Germans because of its ability to outmaneuver and aim its guns at targets. The Sherman tank guns were 30-cal. and 50-cal. machine guns, a bow gun (which could shoot at a forty-five-degree angle), and a 75mm cannon, which was later replaced by a 76mm cannon. The tanks had three-inch thick armor and had a top speed of twenty-five miles per hour with a crew of five men—driver, bow gunner, gunner, loader, and commander. The cannons fired armor piercing and exploding incendiary shells. The German tanks had heavier gauge steel armor, whereas our tanks had to be closer to inflict damage to their tanks because many shells from a distance would simply bounce off their armor.

"Tank destroyers were highly effective with great speed and gave a good account of their actions. They had light armor to protect them from machine gun, fragmentations and rifle fire. They should have been used sparingly, but when needed, they were used against tanks. They were like a cat going after a dog."

Finally, the Division crossed into Germany. It was split into three combat commands—Combat Command A (CCA), Combat Command B (CCB) and Combat Command Reserve (CCR). Each fought well. A Combat Command usually consisted of a company of infantry, six tanks, a reconnaissance platoon and an engineer platoon. Combat Commands A and B normally traveled parallel to each other, and the Reserve brought up the rear and went wherever needed. When planning an attack, the commander of each combat command requested the number of engineers, artillery, etc. that he needed.

Philip recalled, "Our platoons and/or companies were assigned as required. One time, we might be in CCA, next time in CCB, or if we were lucky, CCR. I was in command of Company C, Ninth Armored Engineer Battalion. We traveled fairly rapidly and without too many problems. In most of the small towns, we saw white sheets hanging out every window. If no one fired on us, we went through town without hassling the German residents. If any firing came from a town, we leveled it with tank and artillery fire.

"To this day, I still remember one incident clearly as we entered a small town. I was in one of my half-tracks and about three or four vehicles from the lead. A reconnaissance vehicle led the column and came face to face with a German Army truck. The soldiers in the reconnaissance vehicle fired a high explosive round through the truck. As we all continued to move past the truck, we could see that the canvas had been blown off the truck's side, and as we passed, we saw two children about eight or nine years old dying in the back of the truck. I think I threw up. We didn't stop."

CHAPTER 10

The Remagen Bridge

✦✦✦

As platoon commander, Philip felt responsible for his men. These men were under his care, and he formed a bond with them. His men respected and liked him, and he was well liked by his fellow officers. On March 6th, one day before the Remagen bridge capture, Philip's commanding officer sent his wife, Valerie, a letter.

Dear Mrs. "High-Explosive" 6 March 45

The name we pinned on "Bish" goes on to you- the reason being he gets such a terrific kick out of anything that shoots, anything that explodes. Now that he's an engineer- we have plenty that does just that. He's a real guy, "gal", and no doubt you're plenty proud of him and you have plenty reason to be so. Everyone in our company really likes the guy and I personally am thankful he came to our outfit when he did. Wouldn't part with him for the world. Of course, like all the rest, he always wants to know when he's going home – honestly, a real crew here and you sure want to meet the boat cause you'll be able to hear us coming.

Looking forward to meeting you. Best of luck always.

The "Ol' Man"
Capt. Ellis G. Fee

On the morning of March 7, 1945, the Americans captured the Ludendorff Bridge at Remagen, Germany. It was a miracle to see the bridge still standing when Second Lieutenant Karl H. Timmermann of Able Company, 27th Armored Infantry Battalion, and his men first caught site of it silhouetted against the gray sky as they approached the old Roman town. They could see German troops and town residents scrambling across the bridge to the east bank. This was an unexpected prize. Up to this point in time, the mission of the Allied Armies was to destroy the German forces west of the Rhine. The capture of the bridge would create a springboard for the Allied Forces to leap across the Rhine to the east into Germany's industrial heartland. Hitler, determined to hold the Siegfried Line at all cost, ordered the destruction of every bridge that spanned the Rhine. As soon as the Germans saw the Americans coming, they detonated a charge they had buried on the west end of the bridge. It blew a thirty-foot crater. It became obvious to the Americans the German Army had wired the entire bridge.

Meanwhile, Philip and the Ninth Armored Engineer Battalion were in the small town of Sinzig situated approximately three or four miles south of Remagen. While Second Lieutenant Timmermann was leading his men towards the town of Remagen, a task force of the Ninth under the leadership of Lieutenant Colonel William R. Prince was attempting to seize the bridge over the River Ahr. In spite of tough opposition, Colonel Prince's task force succeeded in taking the Ahr Bridge before the Germans blew it up.

Philip said, "I was called to the front of the line to determine if our tanks could cross the small bridge at Sinzig. It appeared that it could hold the tanks and I returned to my half-track. Suddenly, the lead tank commander who was still standing near his tank was shot and killed by a sniper. Within seconds, we spotted the sniper hiding in a tree. The gunner in the lead tank swung his 90mm gun and shot the sniper along with destroying most of the tree. A few minutes later, I saw a German command car streaking away from town. I began firing the 50-cal. machine gun, but before I had a good bearing, the Germans disappeared over a small hill."

Colonel Prince's task force not only took the bridge, but also captured four hundred prisoners. They also rounded up some Volkssturms (national militia Germany established toward the end of the war of males between the ages of sixteen to sixty who were not serving in a military unit) and any civilians who didn't appear friendly. Two of the civilians indicated they had valuable information they wanted to pass on to the American authorities. An intelligence officer interrogated them, and learned the German command planned to blow up the Remagen bridge at 4:00 p.m., on the dot. It was now half past two. The intelligence officer immediately sent a priority radio message to Combat Command B headquarters alerting them of the urgent information. The Combat Command relayed it on. Knowing there was not a minute to waste, and fearing that the message may pass through several channels, the intelligence officer dispatched a special messenger to carry the news to Colonel Engeman, the commander who was spearheading the Ninth Armored Division's drive toward the Rhine.

Information coming from a citizen, wouldn't necessarily be accurate. *Could a citizen have access to such detailed information of a military plan?* Later, the German troops captured at the bridge, swore there was no set hour to blow the bridge. Rather, they had planned to blow it upon the appearance of the

American forces. True or not, the news triggered the American commanders and troops into quicker action to secure the bridge before the Germans could destroy it. When General Hoge, the commanding general of Combat Command B, received the message, it was already 3:15 p.m., so, he immediately went into action. The German Army had wired the bridge to blow once the order was given, but only a portion of the explosives detonated, and the Ludendorff was still standing. To prevent the bridge from being blown, General Hoge ordered the engineers to pull out the detonation wires around it and ordered tanks and machine guns to give them cover. He further ordered them to fire off some white phosphorous and smoke around the area to screen their activity. The Americans took control of Remagen and the west end of the bridgehead, and were determined to take the bridge intact. Though they knew the bridge could be blown to pieces at any moment, the engineers, under heavy fire, rushed onto the bridge to cut the wires connected to the detonator and threw hundreds of pounds of explosives into the Rhine. The German soldiers fought furiously to prevent the Americans from taking the bridge while it was still intact. The German troops used every weapon at their disposal, including aircraft, to destroy it, but failed. It was a bloody aggressive battle that continued for several days.

The American soldiers succeeded in capturing the Ludendorff before it was destroyed, but not without being exposed to heavy machine gun fire. The capture of the bridge was the first allied bridgehead to be established across the Rhine since the time of Napoleon. This unplanned military success changed the course of the war.

"We were to stay in Sinzig for several days," said Philip, "so my platoon placed a roadblock on the south end of town to stop enemy tanks which were down the river. Then we were to turn south and go down the Rhine River until we closed a circle with the Germans locked in. My platoon took possession of a nice little hotel that had been occupied by German officers. After we placed the road block, we went back to the hotel. When the Germans had sat down to eat, they found out they were about to have *guests* and evacuated. There was food still on the table when we arrived. The waiters were around so we just put them to work for us. We were very happy in our new home, but it didn't last long because I received a call on the radio. It was late at night, and we were ordered to head up the river to Remagen. Combat Company B had captured the Ludendorff Railroad Bridge at Remagen and it was still intact. The infantry force beyond the Rhine needed rapid reinforcement if it was to survive the next few crucial hours. We were to cross the Rhine River."

The commanders involved scrambled to assemble as many troops and as much equipment they could possibly scrape together to send to the west bridgehead. This was a monumental task. To add to the difficulty, the road eastward into Remagen was in poor condition and the increased load of troop traffic jammed it.

Meanwhile, back at the Ludendorff Bridge, the armored engineers, under the direction of Lieutenant Hugh Mott, worked at top speed to prepare the bridge ready to accommodate the military vehicles. Finally, about midnight Mott gave the all-clear signal to Lieutenant Engeman to send his tanks over. The infantry that made it across to the east side of the river was on its own until reinforcements could cross over the bridge. They had already fought off several German small-scale counterattacks, and were nervous about spending a dark night without tank support.

The night was black and rainy. The engineers strung white tape along the bridge to create the best visibility possible, and also roped off the large crater-like holes in the planking. Four thirty-five ton tanks lumbered across the bridge to the other side without a problem. Five more tanks followed the white tape to the east side of the Rhine. Next, they wanted to get some tank destroyers across the bridge. Since tank destroyers aren't as heavy as the General Sherman tanks that had crossed over, the first destroyer started out a little faster than the Sherman tanks. The destroyer was doing well until three quarters of the way across when it came to one of the huge holes in the flooring caused by a German emergency demolition. Unfortunately, the right tread of the destroyer fell into the hole. The crew wasn't harmed and climbed out to see what happened. Though it was pitch dark, they realized the destroyer was hanging on its side unsteadily balanced over the Rhine. Now the bridge was blocked, allowing only soldiers on foot to cross the bridge. The soldiers of the armored infantry battalions had no choice but to leave their vehicles on the Remagen side. The engineers tried to right the destroyer, but couldn't budge it. They tried crowbars, pushing and pulling with other vehicles, and jacking up the suspended destroyer to no avail. They labored for hours and decided to try pushing the destroyer into the Rhine. That didn't work either. Although the destroyer seemed to be hanging by a thread, it couldn't be budged. Finally, at five-thirty in the morning they succeeded in dislodging the monster vehicle and towed it away, freeing up the bridge passageway for the backed-up traffic behind. They suffered and labored through the night and into the morning of March 8th.

The nine tanks that made it across the bridge were dispersed along the 3,500 yard frontage of the bridgehead. Without additional support, they would be in a vulnerable position to defend themselves through the night. Because of the darkness, enemy soldiers on foot could approach undetected to fire their rocket launchers at close range.

"As we approached Remagen, a jam-up on the bridge had us stopped in the middle of the road about a quarter of a mile away. It was late at night on March 7th, around eleven o'clock. I was in a half-track along with five or six soldiers. I assigned a guard to stay awake because there were too many Germans in the area. We tried to sleep, we were tired as hell. I was worried because I knew the countryside was swarming with German soldiers. My guard promptly went to sleep so I stayed awake. At dawn, I saw Germans by the dozen coming through the woods. They had surrendered and were in a column of fours with their hands in the air. We motioned them back down the road to our rear. Some troops behind us took care of the prisoners.

"Later in the morning, we started on up and got to the edge of the bridge. The Germans had blown a chunk out of it so we couldn't move forward. We were in a jeep and being shelled heavily. My driver and I jumped out of the jeep and took cover behind a large cement post. We sat there about fifteen or twenty minutes until finally the column started to move."

Shells were falling, artillery whizzed overhead, and guns fired. The bridge and anyone on it was a target. Under fire, Philip's driver pushed the gas pedal of their jeep and they dashed across the entire two-hundred-fifty yards of the bridge without incident. Another lieutenant in his unit wasn't as lucky. His driver's head had been blown off by a shell. Blood flew all over the lieutenant. He went completely mental. He jumped from his jeep and ran into the railroad tunnel on the far side of the bridge.

"No amount of coaching would get him out of the tunnel. They had to get an ambulance in there and strap him in, and ship him away. As he left us, he was certainly insane. We never saw him again."

Men died that day crossing the bridge. Philip saw both American and German bodies being dragged off the bridge and put into the railroad tunnel.

Several days after they crossed, Philip found that his barracks bag which had been in the back seat of his jeep was shot with shrapnel. When he opened it, and unrolled his socks, it looked like mice had been in them. He realized how lucky he was and thought, *other folks weren't so lucky.*

"We stayed east of the Rhine River for about a week. We lived In a huge house with walls lined with bottled wine, cognac, rum, and other intoxicants. Handy *encouragement.* We needed it. We as officers took turns inspecting the bridge for shell damage while under extreme artillery fire and air bombings.

The Ludendorff Bridge withstood all enemy action for ten days. Heavy military traffic poured across. When we pulled out on March 16th, an engineer unit with better construction capabilities moved in to make further repairs on the bridge."

The German reaction to the capture of the bridge was violent and intense. They quickly positioned their tanks and infantry to hurl artillery fire at the bridge. Hundreds of Luftwaffe pilots were in the air to bomb it. They floated mines down the river hoping they would hit their target, and sent men on barges loaded with explosives toward the bridge. They failed. The Germans even used trained swimmers clad in rubber suits to tow large, heavy charges of explosives, but failed. The Americans spotted and captured them. With all of these attacks, the bridge remained standing. For the next two weeks, the troops fought bloody battles to hold the center of the bridgehead against repeated Ninth and Eleventh Panzer Division attempts to smash toward the bridge.

On the afternoon of March 17, 1945, at about three o'clock, tragedy struck. The Ludendorff Bridge at Remagen collapsed, sending many Army engineers to death or injury into the swift cold water of the Rhine. Philip and his platoon had pulled out the day before. Had they stayed one day later, Philip and his men would have been working on the bridge during the collapse. The bridge had been closed for repairs except for brief intervals, and no traffic was passing over at the time of the collapse.

Approximately two hundred engineers were working on the bridge when it gave way without warning. Seven engineers of the 276th Engineer Combat Battalion and the 1058th Port Construction and Repair detachment were killed. Eighteen were missing whose bodies were never recovered and three more men subsequently died of their injuries. Twenty-eight men sacrificed their lives, and sixty-three men suffered injuries when they were thrown into the icy waters of the Rhine when the bridge collapsed. The bridge had withstood the bombings, explosions and extensive damage. While weakened, it held the weight of the machinery and men during the repair. One engineer's opinion was that combined with the damage, the bridge collapsed as a result of constant vibrations caused by the various numerous sources—the previous bombings into the river and artillery fire into Remagen, the repair process using air compressors, a crane, trucks, several electric arc welders, and all the hammering. He believed the continued vibrations affected the previously buckled top chord causing it to completely buckle under the heavy load which it was never designed to hold.

The capture of the Ludendorff contributed to hastening the end of the war. This capture caused a serious threat to the heart of Germany, and it became a springboard for the final offensive to come. When Hitler learned about the capture, he was livid with rage. He sought out the commanders in charge of the Ludendorff Bridge to have them court-martialed for their failure to blow the bridge before the Americans captured it. The unfortunate officers who Hitler blamed weren't allowed to have a defense attorney and were judged guilty. They were immediately marched out to the woods with their hands tied behind their back and executed by Hitler's firing squad. When they dropped to the ground, their bodies were tossed into a shallow grave with only a few inches of dirt covering them. The court found five officers guilty and sentenced them to death. Four were in German hands, and the fifth officer who was court-martialed *in absentia*, was a prisoner of the Americans. He was the lucky one.

Years later, the captured officer would give invaluable insight to the German perspective of the battle. In 1969, a movie was made called *The Bridge at Remagen* starring Robert Vaughn, George Segal, Ben Gazzara and Bradford Dillman. The movie-makers shot part of the movie in Czechoslovakia, but they were interrupted in that location by the Soviet invasion in 1968.

After the war, General Eisenhower said it well about the significance of the seizure of the bridge: (Quote taken from the book, *The Bridge at Remagen, The Amazing Story of March 7, 1945—The Day The Rhine River Was Closed,* by Ken Heckler, 1957).

> *Broad success in war is usually foreseen by days or weeks, with the result that when it actually arrives, higher commanders and staffs have discounted it and are immersed in plans for the future. This was completely unforeseen. We were across the Rhine, on a permanent bridge; the traditional defensive barrier to the heart of Germany was pierced. The final defeat of the enemy, which we had long calculated would be accomplished in the spring and summer campaigning of 1945, was suddenly now, in our minds, just around the corner.*

> —General Dwight D. Eisenhower

President Franklin D. Roosevelt, who did not live to see the end of the war, was able to live long enough to witness and share in the elation of this important moment of the war. He died six weeks later on April 12, 1945. The nation and the soldiers overseas mourned the loss of their leader. President Harry Truman took on the monumental task of stepping into President

Roosevelt's shoes in the midst of the war.

Philip said, "Of course, the headlines in newspapers throughout the United States was 'BRIDGE COLLAPSES.' Valerie, my wife, was worried sick because she didn't know I had moved out of the area the day before. One of several close calls with death. I sent a V-Mail to my mother and father."

Dear Mom and Dad,   *12 March 45*

Suppose you already know by now that I am east of the Rhine. My platoon was with the outfit that grabbed the bridge, so I have had a ringside seat. Would have gladly traded my seat for one in the back row plenty of times on this trip, but everything came out ok. I haven't had time to write, wash or anything else lately so keep Val's morale up. Am hoping the Heinies throw in the sponge soon so I can head for home. I am looking both ways so don't worry about me.

Your son
Phil

When Philip and his platoon left Remagen, the once peaceful town was shattered. Had they been able to visit the quiet town of Remagen before the war, they would have found a charming, unhurried and relaxed community. The townspeople enjoyed being able to live along the Rhine River. In fact, it was considered fashionable to live close to the Rhine. Remagen was a resort town that attracted many tourists, who while there, enjoyed the rich scenery of the Rhine area, and the mountains and valleys surrounding it. There were elegant restaurants for dining and hundreds of friendly boutiques for shopping. They would have seen, and perhaps visited, Remagen's proudest shrine—the four-towered Gothic Church of St. Apollinaris which had a history as far back as the Middle Ages. And spanning across the Rhine, they would have seen the stately Ludendorff Railroad Bridge with its three symmetrical arches silhouetted against the sky sweeping toward Erpeler Ley. Four heavy stone towers anchored the bridge with two on the Remagen side and two on the Erpel village side.

The little town showed no signs of modernization. Industrial smoke and noise were nonexistent.

The Ludendorff Bridge was constructed in 1916 for the purpose of enabling the transportation of German troops and supplies from east to west across the Rhine in the event of war.

The American troops in 1945 weren't the first to cross the bridge. Shortly after the Armistice ended the First World War, in December of 1918, the III Corps of the United States Army crossed the Ludendorff over the Rhine River. In contrast to the soldiers in the World War II bridge crossing who used jeeps, half-tracks and tanks, the III Corps used horses.

Now, in March of 1945, the soldiers were leaving a town that had been carpeted with bombs. The daily routine for the populace consisted of standing in line early in the morning with their ration cards for food, and taking their children into the woods to safety by noon before the air-raid sirens screamed the warning. Many people tried to carry on with whatever functions they could still perform among the chaos and rubble. Despite much of the damage which had been inflicted by the Americans, most of the people weren't bitter toward them. They wanted the war to be over, and to be liberated by the Americans.

First sight of the Ludendorff Bridge, March 1945, Remagen, Germany

Tunnel at the east end of the Ludendorff Bridge at Erpeler Ley, Germany, March 1945

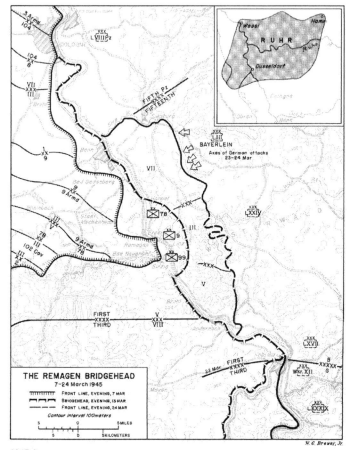

MAP 3

Remagen Bridgehead Map - Germany, March 1945

U.S. First Army at Ludendorff Bridge, Remagen, Germany, four hours before its collapse into the Rhine, March 1945

Ludendorff Bridge, Remagen, Germany, after collapse, March 1945

Ludendorff Bridge, Remagen, Germany, December 1918

CHAPTER 11

The Final Days

✦✦✦✦

Philip recalled, "On the way to Leipzig from Remagen, my platoon remained behind at a small river to perform a task while our company proceeded on. After we were finished, I followed an infantry company that stopped in a fair-sized town, but they advised me to wait for daylight before trying to find my company. The next morning, when we got up, we heard an airplane starting up a couple hundred yards away. I thought the town was in control of the United States, so thought the plane was one of ours. We were standing outside getting ready to leave, when this huge airplane came up over the top of the buildings, approximately fifty to sixty feet above the rooftops. It was a German bomber. I tried to get on the half-track as fast as I could. But we had covered up the 50-caliber machine gun with a tarp to keep the dampness off it, and before I could get it uncovered, the plane was gone. But I often wondered what it would have been like to shoot down a German bomber from the ground.

"I also recall another little job. A roadblock was slowing a unit somewhere ahead and my platoon was to take it out. I checked a map and decided on a shortcut to the work area. Our travels took us through a small town. As we approached, Germans began running. It dawned on me my little platoon was entering an enemy town that had not yet been captured. At every intersection, I sweated out a German unit. We went through town and on the outskirts was a huge fenced area filled with slave workers—all women. When they saw us, they went berserk, screaming and laughing and jumping at the fence. My group wanted to stop and release the mad maidens immediately. I told them we had to go do our job, but we would come back and release the ladies. We never got back."

When Allied soldiers came into a town, the residents used white flags, bed sheets and tablecloths to signal surrender. Soldiers posted copies of General Eisenhower's Proclamation No.1, which began with *We came as conquerors, not as oppressors.* The Proclamation demanded absolute compliance instituting a strict curfew and limited travel, and seized all communication equipment and weapons.

"Our column slowly proceeded through Germany. At times, Germans stood and applauded as we went by. If they shot at us, we shot back. One of our lieutenants had his half-track hit so he slipped out to see the damage. This was a big mistake as a sniper shot him. His wound qualified him to be sent home. A condition many of us would have accepted."

Philip sent a V-Mail to his parents.

Dear Folks,   *4 April 45*

Had a few minutes to drop you a line, but all I could locate was this V-mail. I am getting along fine, eating good, etc. Although sitting right in the middle of the enemy is hard on one's nerves. We nailed five of the vaunted SS Storm troopers yesterday. They aren't supposed to surrender but I let them come until they were looking right into the barrel of a machine gun. That seemed to change their minds somewhat.

The weather has been bad lately. Rains every few minutes. Think we'll have them whipped soon though, and we can take the weather until then. Don't worry. I am fine.

Your son
Phil

By the time they reached Leipzig and lined up along the Mulde River, the war was winding down. In fact, there were hundreds and hundreds of German soldiers walking up toward them with their hands in the air. The soldiers could hear the Red Army's guns and knew the Russians were coming soon. Given a choice, they preferred to surrender to the Americans rather than become prisoners of the Russians. Having reached an agreement with General Eisenhower to avoid a clash of the two advancing armies, the Russians agreed to halt their army at the Elbe-Mulde line. They fully expected to seize Berlin and to clear the Germans from the east bank of the Elbe north and south of Berlin as well as to take Prague. On April 25, 1945, this historic meeting would take place between unexpected comrades in arms fighting the same enemy.

For Philip, his experience in the Mulde River area would hold a lasting impression. He would never forget the near miss of the sniper bullet meant for his head. In contrast to that close call, he came upon the rare opportunity to billet in the medieval Castle Puchau of the Von Hohenthal family. It was typical when troops entered a town and the surrounding area, for the officers to pick out the nicest residence as their *headquarters*. It was up to the officer whether to request the owners to leave their home, and usually on short notice. They allowed the owners to take a few belongings with them, and were on their own to find another place to live. Philip didn't plan to ask the owners to leave. He did, however, arrange to have all of their weapons removed. They had an entire wall covered with collectible guns. The residents of the castle were a German count, his wife, a countess, and their daughter, also a countess.

"I was pretty much in clover. I visited my troops on one of the Count's horses. All I had to do was speak and my desires were addressed. The kitchen staff sent my meals with a bottle of booze to my room. My sergeants and I usually took care of a bottle. When we fired mortars at the Germans, our aiming was not good so we hit very little."

Philip assumed the Count was a wealthy German citizen, but he was not who he appeared to be. The Count always disappeared whenever the Americans were present. At the beginning, the family was fearful to have American soldiers living with them, but after a few days, the Countess came to trust Philip. He had developed a rapport with her and they even discussed how much they both liked hunting, and, before all the guns had been removed, the Countess gave one of her hunting rifles to Philip as a gift. Later, he shipped the gun back to the states.

One day she approached Philip and confided that she had a matter of great concern to discuss with him. She revealed that her husband was a colonel in the Germany Army. Not only was he a colonel, but he was one of Hitler's key officers. She and her husband were in a state of panic because he wasn't wearing his uniform when Philip took over their house. The Countess explained that her husband knew his country was losing the war and had abandoned his position. He made the decision to go home to be with and protect his family, and was now caught out of uniform. What should they do? Philip responded, "Tell him to put that uniform on immediately!" The colonel donned his uniform knowing he would become a prisoner, but it was preferable to be taken as a prisoner than to be taken as a spy. He descended the stairs in a stately manner and formally surrendered to Philip, and handed over his pistol, handle first. Philip had no choice but to take him to the prisoner area. "The headquarters staff was happy to see him since he was one of Hitler's big shots," Philip said, "And the colonel was quite cooperative in providing information."

The young countess carried her own burden, and came to Philip. She told him she was so afraid of the Russian army that she had considered committing suicide. She begged Philip to take her with him. He explained it just wasn't possible. He talked her out of taking her life and told her at least they could feel assured that while the Americans were there, the family would be safe.

The family had good reason to be afraid. The Russians did arrive, and once Russia took control of Eastern Germany, the Hohenthal family and many other nobles lost their castles and land. They became victims of the Stalinist land reform act beginning in 1945 to 1949. Their property was seized, and they were forced to leave with minimal belongings and none of their possessions. The Hohenthals had owned their property for 150 years, and it was suddenly snatched away.

Soon another company arrived to meet up with the Russians, so Philip and his men left the Leipzig area to advance toward the German *redoubt* (a designated location to make a last stand). Hitler gave orders that the soldiers *were not to surrender, and they were to fight to the death*. Those who committed to following the Fuhrer's orders, rushed to the redoubt for a last stand.

"The area was swarming with Germans. We expected a stiff defense to the death. When we arrived, we waited for the order to attack at 10:00 a.m., but the order never came. Silence. Then we received word the war was over, and the Germans had surrendered." It was May 5th, 1945.

Far from the battlefield, Hitler and his wife had holed up in his underground bunker of his headquarters in Berlin. He was paranoid about being captured by the Russians. Reports were rampant that Adolph Hitler, the man responsible for millions of deaths and the destruction of so many European cities, bit into a cyanide pill, pressed his service pistol to his head, and shot himself. It was April 30, 1945. His wife, Eva Braun, also killed herself by taking cyanide.

Two days beforehand, on April 28th, Mussolini was captured by Italian partisans and put to death.

The German armies in Italy surrendered on May 2nd, and on May 5th, V-E (Victory in Europe) was announced.

On May 8, 1945, back in the United States, President Truman gave a broadcast to the American people, and said, "The flags of freedom fly over all Europe."

"Each soldier went home according to a point system. The soldiers who had been in the longest had enough points stacked up to go home. I didn't have quite enough points, so I stayed behind in the unit while some of the guys shipped out. We were stationed in a German town waiting to go home. Within minutes, and I mean only minutes, German girls appeared when we arrived. They surrounded us, and the troops didn't mind.

"One night, I was rousted from my little sack by Captain Lee, our company commander. He told me that something had occurred down the street and an American officer was needed. I dressed and proceeded to the area. At the time, we required the Germans to be locked in their buildings, and not to come out after dark. I went down, and there were Germans hanging out their windows pointing at a door. I opened the door and walked into a pool of blood. An elderly German man, shot through the head and dead, was lying in the middle of the blood.

"We were the only combat unit in town, and the only people who had guns. It was obvious someone in our little organization had done this German in. The war had been over for about ten days. I picked up an M-1 rifle casing and went back to our company. I told the Captain one of our soldiers had killed a German civilian. He woke the rest of the platoon and told us to check our men. I found one of my best sergeants passed out drunk, and when I checked his rifle, it was missing one round. The rest of the men in his squad said he had been in bed all night so I continued to check my men. Fifteen or twenty minutes later, one of my sergeants came to me and said they lied and Sergeant S had gone out with his rifle. He was gone for about twenty minutes before returning, and passed out on his bunk dead drunk. Of course, I knew my man had committed the murder. He said he didn't remember anything.

Philip learned that a woman was involved. Although she was married, she set her sights on the young drunk American soldier. She dressed to attract and seduce men. Philip said, "She was a real looker with the shortest skirt I had ever seen." The soldier, who was drinking to celebrate the end of the war, was an easy target. In his drunken stupor, he set out to kill her husband. He forced a German man to kneel on a step, and shot the man between the eyes. But the man he shot, wasn't her husband. He was an elderly German man who had no connection to the woman.

"I called Battalion headquarters and told them what a great soldier my man had been. The prosecutor said there wouldn't be a court-martial. A week or so later, that status changed and there was to be a court-martial. A few days passed, Sergeant S returned to our unit. He had been found not guilty. It seems he had a twin brother in Germany. His brother was brought to the trial and paraded before some German witnesses. All identified him as the shooter. Then they brought in Sergeant S. So, through this phony little fluke because of the fact the war had only been over a few days, they discharged the guy and turned him loose. I told him I didn't ever want to see him drinking again, and he said he was through with drinking.

"Eight years later, in 1953, when I was Company Commander of A Company, 82nd Airborne Division, I received notice of an assignment of a new Master Sergeant to my company. When he arrived, I immediately recognized him. It was Staff Sergeant S, the same dude who shot the German. He was now a Master Sergeant and a master jumper. We had a little talk and I informed him that he and I were going fishing. After we got out into the middle of Lake Mott, a small lake on the reservation, I brought up the past. I wanted to know whether he had quit drinking since he had killed the German while he was so drunk and didn't even remember doing it. He said he quit drinking the day of the incident. I told him his past would stay in the past, and the incident would stay between us. None of the troops would know about it, and that's the way it was. From then on, he was one of my best platoon sergeants, and we never went fishing nor talked about the past again."

CHAPTER 12

Coming Home

✦✦✦✦

The war was over, and some men were coming home, but they were no longer the same men they once were when they left the shores of their homeland. War changes a man. Philip never forgot what he had seen.

"On the battlefield, I saw brave men dying! I saw them crying! I saw mangled bodies! I saw the hungry children! I saw abused people and battle-fatigued soldiers! I saw the misery in concentration camps! I saw happy faces of a well-accomplished mission! I saw boys become men! War is hell for what it does to life and property. Men fought to kill, to maim, to destroy. Some returned home, others remained behind forever on the fields of their greatest sacrifice. There was a war, a great war, and now it was over. I had spent two years fighting the war. Take a combination of fear, anger, hunger, thirst, exhaustion, disgust, loneliness, homesickness, and wrap that all up in one reaction and you might approach the feelings a fellow has fighting a war. It makes you feel mighty small, helpless and alone."

Philip felt fortunate to be one of the men coming home. He had been gone for two years and Valerie wrote to him daily. When Philip came home, he and Valerie reunited on a street corner of New York.

"That little house was going to look like a palace to me. Was it true that people ate three meals a day or more? And they sat on a chair, by a table? There were times I would have traded my soul for a drink of cold water, or a cup of hot coffee. I was to be discharged from the Army in Indiantown Gap, Pennsylvania. Without knowing it, my career as a professional soldier would be decided there. When I went in for my discharge, they asked me to join the Army Reserves. My comment was, 'you guys must be crazy.' I wanted out. Period!"

"Well then", they said, "you have to go to a lecture in the afternoon."

"What if I sign up?"

"You can leave immediately," they said.

"So, I signed up for the Reserves and left camp. That signing got me about ten percent more on my pension and saved my officer status although at that moment I thought I'd seen the last of the U.S. Army. Valerie and I went west to Boise, Idaho. I was looking forward to seeing Idaho again and the *Wild West*."

Valerie was impressed with her first view of Boise. She received a warm welcome from Philip's father while his mother was busy showing Valerie pictures of Philip's old girlfriends and how rich he could have been if only he had married *Zoe*.

The newly reunited couple drove to Lewiston to meet the rest of the relatives including Philip's grandfather. When they returned to Boise, their first priority was to find a place to live and a job. Neither was easy to find so they stayed with Philip's folks.

Philip's first civilian job was as a salesperson for J.C. Penney, but it was in Weiser, Idaho. The newlyweds moved to Weiser, but weren't able to find a house to rent right away. During their search, they learned about a room being available with the Chief of Police. It was the best option available so they took the room. Ironically, the Chief needed a night officer, and persuaded Philip to take the job. The pay was better, but it didn't take long for Philip to find out that wandering around Weiser from 11:00 p.m. to 8:00 a.m. wasn't much fun.

One Saturday evening, an ex-serviceman set in motion an old-fashioned *Wild West* holdup at the Athena Club. The only difference was that he used a taxicab instead of a horse to make his getaway. First, he herded the patrons of the club into a cloakroom and locked them in. Then he forced the manager at gunpoint to hand over about one hundred thirty-five dollars from the cash register and marched the manager to the rear of the club to unlock the door leading to the alley. The robber took the key with him and locked the door from the outside. The singer of the orchestra at the club managed to slip away and ran out into the street to get help. She saw Philip down the street and told him about the robbery. The Deputy Sheriff and Philip responded, and watched for the robber to exit from either the front or side door since they knew the rear door was seldom used and remained locked. The Police Chief arrived on the scene and entered the club only to discover that the robber had used the back door. The robber dashed down the alley to the Washington Hotel where he hired a taxi cab driver to take him to Payette. The robber, who seemed perfectly at ease, remarked to the cab driver, "There seems to be considerable excitement in the town tonight." Payette police received a tip that the robber was headed their way in a cab. A Payette officer waited for the robber's arrival, and upon his arrival, took the robber into custody and held him in the city jail until the Deputy Sheriff and Philip arrived to take him back to Weiser.

Philip and Valerie were expecting their first child. They

decided to go back to Boise where Philip found a job as a field representative for Blue Cross of Idaho.

Tragically, because of an inefficient doctor, Philip and Valerie lost their baby. When Valerie's water broke, she immediately went to see the doctor. He told her to go home and wait, and if nothing happened by the next evening, she should go to the hospital. Nothing happened, so she went to the hospital. Her labor pains started later that evening which continued into the following morning. The baby was coming. Valerie heard the nurses trying to call the doctor, and heard one mention the Country Club. In the meantime, the nurses told her to quit pushing while they held her legs together. On August 28, 1946, Valerie gave birth to a full term 8 lb. 2 oz. stillborn baby girl. They named her Bonnie. The doctor's reason for the death was that the cord was wrapped around the baby's neck and she suffocated. It was a tough time for the devastated young couple. They refused to pay the doctor and consulted a lawyer about suing for negligence, but the attorney said it would be a difficult case and recommended not suing. Philip's boss, R.T., suggested they might feel better if they left Boise. He offered to transfer them to Wallace, Idaho. But what should they do about the house they had just agreed to purchase? R.T. was a generous and compassionate man. He bought the house from them and made all the arrangements for their move. All they had to do was pack their clothes and drive to Wallace. When they arrived at Wallace, they found a furnished apartment in a fourplex which they rented on the spot.

CHAPTER 13

Time For A Change

◆◆◆◆

On April 29, 1948, Valerie gave birth to a healthy baby girl weighing 9 lbs. 2 oz. at the Wallace Hospital. They named her Linda Jane. Their life was about to change. It had been just the two of them, and now there were three. They had always spent their leisure time playing cards with their friends, the Winans, as well as going on picnics and fishing. The Winans' son, Dan, was born in December of 1948, and they all planned for Linda Jane and Dan to get married someday.

The Bishops spent over two years in Wallace, but Philip's job was slowly going downhill. They went back to Boise with plans to purchase a small house and to settle down. Philip found a job selling punchboards to taverns which involved traveling throughout Idaho. The punchboard was a gambling device. For twenty-five cents, the player punched out a piece of paper that had a number on it. The number indicated what prize they won or, didn't win. The job was commission only, but he was making four to five hundred dollars a week, about twice the normal work wage. He was drinking a lot, too, since his customer base was mainly the tavern.

Philip first began drinking at the age of sixteen. It started at a church party when a girl he liked invited him to a party. She said, "Please don't drink anything." Up to that point, he had never had a drink. She invited his friend, Bill, to the same party as well.

"We met to go to the shindig and Bill had a pint of moonshine. Someone had dug up a ten-gallon barrel hidden in a cemetery. Bill helped himself to a pint. He and I drank the pint before we arrived to the church party and when we arrived, we were both drunk as skunks. We tried playing Ping-Pong and when the ball went under a chair, I managed to get my head stuck under the chair. In the meantime, Bill was in a fistfight with his brother over a necktie that Bill was wearing. By this time, my so-called girlfriend wasn't speaking to either of us, and we were both thrown out of the party. I didn't want to go to Bill's house, so I went to the fire station and crawled up into the seat of the fire engine. I rang a few bells and Fritz, my dad's brother, John Alfred Bishop, came downstairs, took a look at me, and started laughing. I spent the night in the fire engine and the next morning throwing up. Years later, I would reflect back about Fritz in a much different way."

After the church party experience, Philip thought he would never take another drink again. Not so. For the next ten years, he drank periodically, but it was always more, and more. While he was overseas, especially where they confiscated booze, it was easy to drink a lot, and he did. Everybody did, it seemed. One time when they were going to be used as Infantry to attack a small town, their S-4 issued everyone a quart of pink champagne that he had procured. They drank it of course. A few days after the war was over, Philip spotted a railroad tank car with a group of Germans around it. He checked it out and found the car held 5,000 gallons of cognac. He put a guard on the valuable cargo of potent booze. Everyone in their company had at least one five-gallon can, and before they left the area, each had ten gallons. Their military headquarters in Paris heard about their find and called to see if they could get some of the liquor. They sent a truck from Paris to Hof, Germany, and took back five hundred gallons.

When Philip returned home from the war, his brother-in-laws, also heavy drinkers, took him to the Polish clubs where they lived it up. The civilians always bought the welcomed soldiers drinks, and when that died out, they started buying their own. He wasn't out of control with his drinking habit until he started the punch card job of selling to all the taverns and bars. He even drank in the morning when he wasn't feeling well reasoning that a drink would make him feel better. By the time his and Valerie's daughter, Bettie, was born on May 26, 1949, at the Boise Hospital, Philip was drinking every day. Valerie didn't pressure him about it, but he was sure she wasn't happy.

Philip said, "I was never mean nor nasty, just drunk. I was selling in Northern Idaho and sometimes I was away from home for a week. On one particular instance while I was in Northern Idaho, I was experiencing a bad hangover and got very shaky. I was writing an order, but my hands shook so badly the owner insisted I take a drink. I stayed in that bar for two days. I called Valerie to tell her I was back. The problem was, I had called her two days earlier to tell her the same thing. So, she knew I was on a big drunk. She called my father, and he called the Spokane AA and two guys showed up to my hotel room. They asked if I wanted to go with them to AA or stay drunk. I opted to go with them. As we passed the bar, I took one double shot of whiskey and that was the last drink I ever took.

"One guy drove my car, and I rode with the other one to Spokane where we went to a hotel, called the DT Hotel. I thought it stood for *Delirium Tremors*, but it actually meant downtown. I still remember the hotel clearly today and have never forgotten it. Quitting liquor was rough. I spent five days in Spokane. I couldn't eat or drink anything. When I tried, it immediately came up. The DT hotel was actually an AA meeting place. After about the second day, we had to start going to meetings. I was sick, sweating, and in general, feeling like I wanted to die. I looked over at another dude, who was as sick as I was, and if I hadn't felt so bad, I might have laughed."

In December of 1949, when Philip quit drinking, he started thinking about a future. He had a wife and two children now to provide for. He decided that sales weren't for him. He had been a soldier for six years, so he went to the recruiter and asked them about the regular Army. The recruiter told Philip he could get him on as a staff sergeant. He and Valerie decided that would be the best plan. They sold their furniture they had just started to accumulate, rented the house out, packed up the station wagon, and in the midst of winter, drove to Fort Belvoir, Virginia, where Philip would be an instructor. He taught demolition and mine warfare. He happened to meet a colonel whom he had worked for at Fort Lewis when the colonel was a captain at the time, and Philip was a private. He offered Philip instant Master Sergeant if he would join his unit which was training in Korea. In response, Philip asked for a transfer, but was told all instructors weren't to be transferred. He wasn't happy about that at the time, but it probably saved his life.

In June of 1950, North Korea had invaded the South. By September of that year, the United States joined and led the United Nations forces to defend the South, and aggressively advanced into North Korea. The American-led UN forces failed to conquer North Korea. With the country still divided, the United States military forces remained in South Korea. The bloody war would continue for two years.

When the Bishops were expecting their third child, they moved to an apartment in Alexandria, Virginia. On April 27, 1951, William Edward, weighing 8 lbs., 5 oz., was born at Fort

Belvoir Hospital. They decided three children were enough, so Philip had a vasectomy procedure done. No more pregnancies.

CHAPTER 14

Paratrooping

With trouble still brewing in Korea, Philip was recalled as a First Lieutenant. He decided that in order to avoid RIF'S (Reduction in Force), he would become a paratrooper since engineer troopers were in demand. This was one of Philip's better decisions since after the Korean War, thousands of officers were let go. He stayed on as an officer because he was a parachuting engineer, a scarce group.

Philip wasn't in very good shape from the days as an instructor standing at the podium.

"Well, said Philip, "I'll get six weeks' notice prior to paratrooping training and then I'll get in shape. Wrong! One Friday, I was notified that I was to appear the following Monday at Fort Benning for parachute school. The first week was all physical, and did I hurt.

"The second week was jump week and I really thought I'd been thrown out of training. It happened like this. We were required to wear dog tags for every jump and on the third morning, I had forgotten mine. I asked the First Sergeant of the company I was in if he had a stray pair. He found one with the name Sergeant Vieca or some other Mexican name. I was wearing a tin with the label Lt. Bishop, and I had Vieca's dog tags. On the first check, I flashed the dog tags and got by. We jumped, and then lined up for jump number two. I flashed my tags, but the checker reached out and read them. He looked at the tags and then at my tin hat and called the major in charge. He was quite mad, apparently because I'd foxed them the first time. His words still haunt me to this day, 'Take off your chute, you are through.' I went back to the company and told the company commander what happened. He said the Major was a hot head and he would probably change his mind. Shortly thereafter, the phone rang and I received an order to be on the 6:00 a.m. flight with a chute on and ready to jump. I was to go out with the wind dummy plane from which they threw out a dummy to check the wind drift in order to dump the troops later. I was the dummy and the Major was in the plane. He told me the plane would make one pass over the jump area and I could either jump when I felt like it or I could sit in my seat and return to the field. No one told the pilot that a real body was going out so he never slowed the plane down as in a regular jump. I jumped, of course, and my crotch hurt for a week. There was a jeep waiting to take me back so I assumed they knew I would jump."

After parachute school, Philip was assigned to the 50th Airborne Regiment Combat Team as an executive officer. He had applied for Russian language school since the Russians appeared to be the next problem for the United States. He received a notice from Washington offering two choices for his next assignment. The choices were to go to Korea or go to Polish language school. He chose the language school. In September of 1952, orders came for the Army Language School located in Monterey, California. The orders were pending for some time. Philip and Valerie had hoped to take their vacation in Idaho that summer. But if the orders for the school came, they would be going that direction anyway, so they would cancel their vacation.

The orders finally came through, and with very little notice to prepare to move, they were all packed and in the car on their way to California. They enjoyed their year in Monterey, but Philip considered the school to be one year of hell. He studied every night and every day and graduated. An Army Language School Festival was held at graduation in May of 1953. Each class had prepared a program. Philip took part as a dancer at a Polish wedding for the Polish class.

Their next adventure took them to Europe. Philip left for Germany two weeks after graduation. The families had to stay behind and waited up to six months before going overseas. Valerie and the children, Linda, Bettie and Bill, moved back to Boise, Idaho, and lived in an apartment a few blocks from Philip's parents. Valerie didn't have a car, so she often depended on them for help. Each Saturday she and the children went to town on the bus, shopped a little, had lunch, then went back home on the bus. This was a training session to condition the children for their upcoming long journey overseas to be with their father. It worked. They were the best behaved and polite travelers. Valerie was proud of them.

Valerie received their port of call in November. Soon the family would be reunited. Bill was age two, Bettie was four, and Linda was five. Their grandfather was sad and nervous when he put them on the train for New York. Their trip on the ship took five days, two of which were stormy. They stayed in their room. Valerie was on the verge of seasickness, but the children were fine and having fun watching things roll from one side of the room to the other.

They arrived in Bad Nauheim, Germany. The family was together again. Philip was now a captain and the post engineer. It was a good assignment for him. He had at one time 1,100 Germans working for him. All he had to do was hint about his needs and whatever it was, it appeared. He felt like a king.

Their first year in Germany was fun and exciting. They explored the country and made some trips to Denmark, Holland and the Netherlands, and also went across the border to Austria. They were living the good life. They had a full-time maid leaving Valerie free to do anything she wanted to pursue.

The second year in Germany became a normal everyday routine. They were beginning to miss the United States, and counted the days when they could go home.

They went back to the States in the late fifties. As they boarded the ship, the band played *Auf Wiedersehen*, a sentimental farewell song, but to Philip and Valerie it was a happy time as they knew they would soon hear *Hello America*. When the family arrived in New York, they took a taxi to pick up their car that had been shipped over, and took some time to have a New York experience. They spent a few days visiting Valerie's relatives in Pennsylvania, then they were off to their next station, Fort Bragg, North Carolina. Philip went to the 82nd Airborne. He was given Company A of the 307th Airborne Engineers. It was a good company and Philip loved his job.

During this time, the Division went to Texas for a big maneuver known as *Exercise Longhorn*. They mobilized for this jump at San Angelo, Texas. While there, one of their troops soloed an airplane, ran it down the runway and into the fence. He jumped out and ran, and was never caught.

Philip recalled another incident, "While waiting for the jump, one of the troopers in our vehicle was involved in an accident near the Mexican border. I was sent to investigate the incident, and to go into Mexico to Villa Acuna, to get two of our Airborne soldiers out of jail. The soldiers had gone across the border and got drunk. During their drunken spree, one of the soldiers hit a prostitute and the other hit a policeman. Hitting the policeman was a mistake and landed both of the soldiers in jail.

One of the soldiers fiercely resisted the arrest, and it took four policemen to restrain him. Because of the soldier's abnormal strength, the sheriff thought surely the soldier must have been on drugs, and was anxious to know the name of the seller. I questioned the soldier and he swore he hadn't taken any drugs, only alcohol. I reported this to the sheriff and told him I believed the soldier, and that our men trained daily in strength building exercises. I got along well with the Mexican sheriff and he released both men to me. I told the men to hit the trail for San Angelo and both beat me back to camp."

On one occasion, they made a practice combat jump that should have been called off because of dangerously high winds. One man was killed and 221 injured. It was apparently the highest casualty rate ever sustained by the group in a jump. One-third of the 221 injured were in serious enough condition to have to remain in the hospital.

The 3,120 men of the regiment jumped in the last phase of *Exercise Longhorn*, a maneuver involving atomic warfare, along with 115,000 men and two Air Forces. Two F-51 fighter planes flying cover for the jump collided and crashed into flames. One pilot was killed and the other pilot bailed out.

A spokesman for *Exercise Longhorn* headquarters announced at 4:00 a.m. that the jump scheduled at Goldthwaite, Texas, seventy miles northwest of Fort Hood, had been called off due to dangerously high winds.

But at 7:15 a.m., they began jumping. The Army Chief of Staff, Air Force Chief of Staff, and Chief of Army Field Forces had come to Fort Hood to see the jump. Since they understood the jump had been postponed, they didn't show up to see it.

Philip described the experience, "The wings of the plane were shaking and the pilots said, 'You'll never jump.' Knowing our company officer, I said, 'I'm sure we will,' and of course we did." They couldn't disappoint the high ranking officials they presumed were there watching.

"When I jumped out of the plane, I could see chutes being blown across the field. As I was trying to land, I had to pull up my feet to avoid a dazed soldier who was standing in my way. When I tried to miss him, I landed on my back. I was dragged for three or four hundred yards until my parachute hit a fence and stopped. I thought for sure my back was broken, but finally I managed to get up. I decided I was hurt and headed over to an area where the medics were waiting. When I got a look at the guys who were really hurt, I staggered on back to where our unit was supposed to be. The next morning I couldn't get out of my sleeping bag. After being lifted out, I tip toed along until I loosened up. This happened for two mornings before I became somewhat normal. I was so beat up, but very lucky that nothing was broken."

Parachuters- Dangerous Jump

Philip as partrooper

CHAPTER 15

Vietnam

+ + + +

In the fall of 1958, Philip received orders to go to Vietnam as an advisor. Once again, Valerie and the children went back to Boise, Idaho. They found a nice home to rent. The day before Christmas, Valerie took Philip to the airport for his one-year tour in Vietnam. It was a sad time for the family.

Philip was assigned to the Military Assistance Advisory Group (MAAG) 7, Bien Hoa, Vietnam. He was there to help train the South Vietnam army.

Life in Bien Hoa was dull. They did have access to a boat and water skis. Philip fell into the Dong Nai River, which was so polluted that he got amebic dysentery and severe hemorrhoids. It was so bad that he had to go to Guam for surgery. When the doctor found out that Philip had amebic dysentery, he cancelled the surgery because if those bugs got into his bloodstream, he would be in trouble. They sent him back to Bien Hoa without the surgery.

They all took turns going to Saigon for the mail. Philip had discovered that bluffing and driving fast was the only way to get through Saigon. He was in fact, a fast and reckless driver. One day, a general saw him and wrote down the license plate number of the jeep Philip was driving. Several days later, a call came from the general's aide in Saigon asking for the name of the driver. Philip's name was submitted, and he was ordered to report to the general. He had gone for the mail on Wednesday, but the date in question was listed as a Saturday. The general had apparently waited a day or two to jot down his observations and had put down the wrong date. That saved Philip. His leader had called the general's aide and told him Philip hadn't been in town on Saturday, and if someone was driving his jeep, that driver was unknown. All the general could do was to cancel the meeting. His mistake saved Philip a fine of two or three hundred dollars. Philip's driving improved after that incident.

Once while water skiing under a bridge, Philip ran into a fish line that was hanging from the bridge. The line ran across his chest until the large hook came up and hooked him in the stomach. The line, which was a thick chalk line, had evidently been in the water for a long time and was completely rotten. Had it been a new line, the hook would have ripped his stomach open and all the polluted water would have entered his intestinal area which would have been deadly.

Philip had an assortment of guns with him, and began hunting for tigers in a jeep at night in the jungle. One night, he hadn't had any luck (he never ended up shooting a tiger, and was happy in later years that he was unsuccessful), and he and his driver were heading back to his quarters when they came face to face with a group of armed Vietnamese men dressed in black wearing conical shaped straw hats. No words were spoken, and Philip and his driver moved on. When Philip arrived back to his headquarters, he told some of the men about the men in black. They replied, "Hey, they were Viet Cong. You were lucky!" Philip had come face to face with Viet Cong terrorists and could easily have been taken prisoner or killed. He was fortunate, because the men in black hadn't been given orders yet to take aggressive action against Americans. But it wouldn't be long.

As far as Philip and his comrades were concerned, July 8,

1959, was just another dull day. But a small force of communist Viet Cong gorillas had plans of its own for that day. The terrorists attacked the U.S. billet during a movie, killing two American military advisors and three South Vietnamese, and wounded one U.S officer.

Philip said, "For eight months I lived over the MAAG 7 dining hall. On the morning of July 8th, I received unexpected and unwelcome transfer orders to Saigon, a fourteen-month duty station fourteen miles from Bien Hoa. Bien Hoa was only a twelve-month duty tour. Feeling extremely irritated, I packed my bags and prepared to move to Saigon.

"Major Buis, an Armor advisor, had been in Vietnam two weeks. He tried hard to get out of Saigon for a shorter duty tour. On this morning of July 8th, he moved into my old room. Major Buis was happy about his transfer. He looked forward to being able to return to his family two months earlier.

"The soldiers of MAAG 7 ate their evening meal promptly at 6:00 p.m. At 6:30 p.m., a Jeanne Crain movie, *The Tattered Dress*, was being shown in the dining room. This schedule never varied, and on this fateful evening, five officers and one NCO (non-commissioned officer) moved back from the table and relaxed for the evening movie. The five officers were Colonel Clay, Major Hallet, Major Buis (the new arrival), Captain Boston and Captain Gorlinsky. Master Sergeant Ovnand was, as usual, elected to run the movie projector. He had just finished writing a letter to his wife in the states and dropped it in the mess hall mailbox. Lieutenant Colonel Davis went to his quarters in another building. Captain Turner went to play tennis, and I jeeped off to my new assignment in Saigon. All personnel of MAAG 7 were present and accounted for.

"The first reel of the movie ran itself out. Captain Gorlinsky flicked on the lights and Sergeant Ovnand began threading a new reel in the machine. Major Hallet laid down on the couch and prepared to sleep through the second reel. Major Buis was sharing pictures of his three young sons with his new buddies.

"Outside, a Vietnamese Army guard, a MAAG cook and an eight-year-old boy stood by the front door watching the movie through the screen door.

"Sergeant Ovnand was still stringing on the new reel when, without warning, automatic weapons fire began pouring into the small room through three open windows. Sergeant Ovnand dropped to the floor groaning. Major Hallet, who had survived five combat wounds in Italy, dived under the table as bullets ripped through the top of the couch. Colonel Clay and Captain Gorlinsky both slid to the floor. Captain Boston started across the room and was hit in the right cheek by a bullet that came out his nose. He dropped to the floor, blood spurting from his torn face. Major Hallet dashed across the room and threw off the lights.

"Outside in the courtyard, the Vietnamese guard dropped with a bullet to the spine. The eight-year-old boy was stitched across the chest with three bullets an inch apart and the cook laid dead from head wounds.

"Sergeant Ovnand tried to stand up and another fusillade of lead ripped into his stomach. He staggered to the stairway and crawled up the stairs. Major Hallet bellied across the floor and sprinted up the stairway. His thoughts were on the guns used by me on a number of futile tiger hunts. In the excitement, he had forgotten my recent exodus. He was in the room before he remembered. Outside the door Sergeant Ovnand rolled over and died. Major Hallet charged back downstairs and slammed out the front door. One of the raiders stood directly in his path. Hallet's fist crashed into the face as he swept past. Jumping into a jeep, the Major shot out of the gravel driveway, driving madly for the Vietnamese Army Garrison area, a mile away.

"Major Buis, badly wounded when he was shot during the first hail of bullets, ran for the back door and into a raider carrying a large home-made bomb. It turned out this raider was one of the Viet Cong I ran into back in the jungle just days before. The bomb exploded between the two men. The explosion blew the bomber completely in half, simultaneously killing Major Buis. Major Buis slid to the pantry floor, his tour finishing exactly five hours after arrival to Bien Hoa.

"As suddenly as it had begun, the firing stopped. The murderers slid back into the darkness and cover of the jungle. Colonel Clay and Captain Gorlinsky lay in the darkness listening to the moans of Captain Boston. Troops from the Army camp began arriving; ambulances and police cars screamed up the driveway. The two Vietnamese guards outside the building were killed in resisting the attack. The eight-year-old son of a Vietnamese cook in the officers' mess was fatally wounded as he watched. Captain Boston was flown to Clark field in Manilla for treatment. The raid of MAAG 7 was over. At this time in Saigon, I sat in an air-conditioned room and wrote to my family: *Due to bad luck, I've been reassigned to Saigon. I may have to remain in Vietnam an extra month.*"

On July 9th as Valerie opened the morning newspaper, she spotted a bulletin notice. *An Army barracks, thirty miles from Saigon was attacked by the Viet Cong. Three were killed and four injured.* She knew this was Bien Hoa and she knew there were only seven Americans stationed there. In her mind, she knew Philip was either killed or injured and she wondered when she would be notified. Philip's dad also read the paper and called to see if she had heard. Names were being withheld. She kept the news from the children, and each time the phone or doorbell rang, she knew it would be her notice. Philip's dad called several times. At 2:00 p.m., he couldn't wait for the evening paper delivery at 5:00 p.m. He went directly to the newspaper office and insisted on getting the names. He called Valerie with news that Philip's name wasn't on the list. She was still puzzled about why he wasn't accounted for. She did feel that somehow, he avoided the attack. Not until a couple of days later when she received Philip's letter did she learn what happened. He was told many times that he would be transferred to Saigon to finish his tour. He resisted because it was an eighteen-month tour. Finally, he received word on the 8th to pack up his gear and get to Saigon, and that someone else had been assigned to his room. He did leave that afternoon and the soldier who took his room was killed.

"And so, the life of a soldier and his family goes on as usual. Since October 22, 1957, this was the first known act of aggression against Americans, U.S. Military advisors, in which American lives were lost. In a letter to my wife, I wrote that the incident appeared to be a *local deal and won't happen again*. Little did I know that this was just the beginning of many years of war with Vietnam in which thousands upon thousands of Americans were killed."

Following is the letter Philip wrote to Valerie and his kids the day after this incident occurred detailing what he understood had happened:

Dearest Vi and kids,   *9 July 59*

Hope you didn't read any news in the paper and have to worry about the Bien Hoa Massacre but anyway I'm still around to write the story. I'm no longer bitching about my Orders to Saigon but am thanking one and all who were responsible.

If you haven't read this in the papers don't let it out as it may be censored but last night the Viet Cong lined up outside our mess hall at Bien Hoa while the movie was on and when the lights came on to change the first reel they let loose through the windows with at least seven automatic weapons and machine guns. Then they came in and threw two large bombs in on top of the mess. The upshot of it all was they killed five out of seven of our detachment. I won't mention their names but my buddy Hallet got away without a scratch and one other officer got away. The rest are dead. As you know by now, I moved on day before yesterday and was reading peacefully in my new room in Saigon. Had it not been for the order, I would have been sitting in the movie with all the rest and I probably wouldn't have any birthday.

This thing has shook me up considerably after living so close to those people for seven months and then missing the deal myself by the grace of God.

The fellow who took my room, and was so happy about it, is dead as hell so you see how lucky I am. The guys didn't have a Chinamen's chance as my quarters were the only ones in the mess with weapons. Any weapons they owned were over in their own quarters so they were helpless. Had I been there and had I been able to make the stairs, I would have had a rifle, a shotgun and two loaded pistols but considering the hail of lead that came in and the surprise of the attack, I don't suppose I could have made it at all.

They won't let me go to Bien Hoa today but an officer who went after told me around three hundred rounds were fired into the one small room plus two bombs and the place is a complete shambles. Apparently it was a well planned operation and they most certainly weren't playing around.

One Viet Cong was killed by his own grenade. I understand he lived in Bien Hoa so his relatives will undoubtedly get some rough treatment today in an effort to find the others. I hope they catch the bastards and put me on the firing squad.

MAAG Hqrs is in a hell of an uproar as these were the first Americans killed here. We are on a condition yellow which *means in effect 'watch your step.' I personally think it was a local deal and will not happen again soon. It has the Vietnamese all shook too. I understand the Vice-President of Vietnam went to Bien Hoa last night and that our entire billet area has a regiment of soldiers around it. Of course, that's slightly late for some of the boys.*

There is of course no cause for worry here in Saigon. We have police on the gate and there are too many people around so don't start worrying.

To me it appears I have a guiding hand looking after me and my extra twenty-five days don't mean much now. I could very easily be coming home tomorrow.

When I see Jack H., I'll get an eyewitness account and tell you all about it.

No other news, as I can't think of much else but this.

All my love,
Phil

CHAPTER 16

Military Retirement

After serving one year in Saigon, Philip came home. He left Idaho to go to Vietnam a few days before Christmas, and now he was due home a few days before Christmas. He boarded the plane in Saigon dressed in a white suit and white shoes and he had a tan that looked like he was from Africa. He intended to change clothes in Seattle, but the plane stopped for only a few minutes and then went straight to Boise. "I received a lot of stares considering I was stepping off into about six inches of snow. I didn't care as I was finally home."

Philip didn't like Vietnam and didn't like advising, but when he came home, he was sent to Kansas City, Missouri, as an advisor to the Reserves. He fought hard against this. His desire was to have his last tour with the Airborne. He was still a captain and would have had a company again. The wheels in Washington said he was too old at the age of forty-four, and so, off to Missouri he went.

Philip hated the whole affair and it got worse. Kansas City was known as a sub sector command and it called for a colonel to run the program. They had a lieutenant colonel when he arrived and they had it pretty good. Then, things suddenly changed. Philip had gone to Fort Leonard Wood to take a short class. While he was there, the sector commander came to visit Fort Leonard Wood and all the officers were required to meet him at the airport. He exited the plane, walked over to the group and asked, "Who is Captain Bishop?" Philip had a short panic attack and answered that he was Captain Bishop. The commander told Philip he was to return to Missouri immediately because he was to be the new sub sector commander. Philip inquired about their lieutenant colonel who was being replaced, but the commander's only answer was that the lieutenant colonel wasn't there anymore and Philip would have to handle it until the colonel's replacement came in. Apparently, their lieutenant colonel had gone AWOL on a big drunk.

Philip said, "I wasn't happy as the company of this type had to play politics with the wheels that were commanding reserve units. If I had known what was in store for us, I'd have been happy to stay as the sector commander. We were easing along when a dude in a suit came marching into my office and put his hand out. 'I'm Mienicke,' he said. I thought he was some unknown reservist and in his civilian clothes, so, I certainly didn't jump up and salute. Unfortunately, he was our new commanding officer, not only a bird colonel, but a paranoid, sick bird colonel. He was the prototype of the know-nothing, midlevel career officer who stayed in during peacetime, waiting to retire because there was nothing out in the real world that he knew how to do. He was extremely unhappy that he was taking over from a captain, namely, me. He immediately started raising hell with everybody with the emphasis on me."

Mienicke continued to unfairly harass Philip and his men. Philip got fed up and started keeping written notes on the colonel's antics. Finally, one day, the colonel made Philip so mad that he said to him, "Colonel, I want to see you in your office."

"What for?", the colonel asked.

"I'll let you know in your office," responded Philip.

After Philip shut the office door, Philip told him he was done taking his abuse and he was going to the Inspector General in

Chicago. The colonel looked a bit shook and informed Philip he had to tell him the reason. Then Philip pulled out his little book of notes and let him have it with both barrels. Since Philip knew he had him, he became even more aggressive.

Later, the colonel called a meeting of his staff and announced that *Phil* (the first time he referred to Philip as anything besides *Bishop*) seemed unhappy about certain things, and proceeded to blame it all on the lieutenant colonel who had always been by the colonel's side. Philip, not wasting a second, stood up in the meeting and said, "Colonel, I'm not unhappy about the lieutenant colonel, I'm unhappy about you." A couple of the officers in the room turned white.

Shortly before Philip's retirement, the lieutenant colonel approached him and said, "The colonel will present you with your retirement papers in a little ceremony."

Philip said, "Wrong! The colonel isn't presenting me with anything. I refuse to salute him and he can kiss my ass!"

After the lieutenant colonel reported back, the colonel called Philip into his office. Philip informed him he wasn't participating in a retirement ceremony.

The colonel said, "You know, Phil, even though you're retired, you could still be court-martialed if you should strike a superior."

Philip agreed that was true. The day Philip retired, the colonel happened to be ill and stayed home from work.

Philip Edward Bishop served his country for twenty years. He officially retired with the rank of Major in June of 1964. For his service, Philip was awarded with the National Defense Service Medal, Armed Forces Reserve Medal, Army Occupation Medal (Germany), and Senior Parachutist Badge. He also received a Citation, Oak ' Leaf Cluster, for Company C, 9th Armored

Engineer Battalion, 9th Armored Division, United States Army.

When Philip was asked later how he felt about the war, he said, "Well, I didn't have any great feelings about the war. It was not anything I sat down and thought about. It was a condition that I was in, and that I was not in it alone. You know there were thousands of us that were in the same bunk, and we were going to be there until the war was over and we just did it, that was all there was to that."

On the day that Pearl Harbor was attacked on December 7th of 1941 by the Japanese, Philip resolved that it was time for him to become a serious soldier to serve his country during its greatest time of need, and continued to serve the United States thereafter until he retired.

CHAPTER 17

Shocking News

◆◆◆

Once retired, Philip was happy to pursue two of his favorite activities—boating and fishing. While he and his family were still in Kansas City, they purchased a seventeen-foot-long boat. Not all went well with the boat nor the four-wheel trailer he purchased to transport the boat easily from lake to lake. It seemed the tires on the trailer were meant for a garden tractor, which accounted for the frequent flats they endured along the busy highways. And of course, there wasn't a spare.

The family enjoyed many years of boating and fishing in spite of all their trials and errors. Philip learned one thing for certain, seamanship was not one of his many accomplishments.

On one trip, Philip's parents accompanied them. They made it to their destination without incident, which they thought was a major accomplishment in itself. Prior to launching their boat, Philip tried to start the motor. "That didn't go well. The motor wouldn't even utter a cough."

Finally, after being completely frustrated and worn out from trying to beat the motor into submission, Philip gave up and they all returned home. Ten minutes after they arrived home, Valerie discovered that Philip had put the wires from the battery in reverse order.

✧ ✧✧

After thirty years of service with the Department of Agriculture in Boise, Idaho, Philip's father retired, and he and Clara moved to Glendale, Arizona.

In May of 1962, Philip received a letter from his father with an update of how they were doing in their new locale. His father reported that he thought he was getting some relief from his arthritis, but his heart had been acting up and he was taking medication for it. He believed he was getting a little better. His appetite was good but he was weak. He and Clara looked forward to visiting their son and the family once he was feeling better.

Two weeks later, on May 19, 1962, Philip's father died at the age of seventy-three. It was a blow for the family, and Philip wanted to comfort his mother by inviting her to live with them in Kansas City, Missouri. She was grateful not to have to live alone in Arizona and accepted the invitation.

All was well until one day Philip got the shock of his life. He made his mother angry at him for some reason, and without thinking, she blurted out something that would change his life forever. A long-held secret was revealed, and it all began in the orchard fields of Lewiston, Idaho.

CHAPTER 18

The Secret

◆◆◆◆

After settling in the lower Snake River area around 1884, Philip's grandfather, John Edward Bishop, began his dream of raising fruit. John Edward and his brothers' efforts were soon rewarded when they discovered fruit flourished in the mild climate of the valley. They raised peaches, apricots, apples, pears, and plums. Life centered around the fruit orchards for John Edward's children, and they knew about hard work. Fruit harvesting during that time was all done by hand which meant hiring hundreds of people to cultivate, irrigate, pick, sort and pack the produce raised to go to market. The work was seasonal, but a person who was willing to hone the *know-how* and be ambitious, could make good money. Wages were twelve to fifteen dollars a month in the summertime and ten dollars in the winter, and room and board was always furnished. The Bishop brothers also dried fruit. To do this, they built a fruit dryer near the river. The building was sixty feet long and was heated by a steam boiler. The center of the building was completely enclosed and was partitioned with slots into which the trays of fruit could be slipped for drying. Along the outside of the building, around the dryer section, the ladies prepared the fruit for the dryer or packed the greener produce for shipping. They dried apricots, peaches, and prunes.

As the years went by, John Edward's sons, Philip Edward,

John Alfred and Charles Fields, now young men, were still working on the fruit ranch when fate stepped in and dramatically affected the lives of two of his sons—Philip and John. With the mix of men and women working on the orchard farm, it wouldn't be a surprise that some of those men and women would get together. John Alfred was no exception. There was a young Irish woman that caught his eye, and she was just as attracted to him. Her name was Delia, and after a brief romantic interlude with John, she became pregnant. Now they had a dilemma. What were they to do? Marriage was an impossibility—Delia was already married. What would they do about the child? Ironically, the solution was close at hand. The other brother, Philip, was married, but he and his wife, Clara, were unable able to have children together. They were thrilled about this unexpected opportunity, and said they would take John and Delia's child to raise as their own. John and Delia were understandably relieved, and agreed to this arrangement. And so, it was mutually agreed that the child would never know who its real parents were, and the family and community would to be sworn to secrecy. Thus, Delia was sent to Salt Lake City where she gave birth to a baby boy on July 9, 1917. Philip and Clara went to Salt Lake City to bring back their son. They named him Philip Edward Bishop, Jr.

The secret in Lewiston Orchards and the Bishop family was well kept. Philip, at the age of forty-five, never knew the truth until that day in 1962 when the secret came out. The woman who was living with Philip and his family was not his mother, but his aunt. His real mother's name was Delia Gertrude Croghan, born in Ireland. And the man he thought was his Uncle John, who worked at the Fire Department, was actually his father. Philip knew his real father (Uncle John) because he grew up near where his *uncle* lived. Unfortunately, John died the year before Philip learned the truth, and so they didn't have the opportunity to bond. He learned he had two half-brothers, John O'Dell Bishop who lived in Salem, Oregon, and Sanford (Sandy) Wayne Bishop in Pendleton, Oregon. Many years passed before Philip and his half-brother would be able to talk about the revelation.

In September of 1992, Philip received an unexpected letter from his half-brother, Sandy.

Dear Phil:

For several years, I have wanted to contact you but I have hesitated doing so as I would never want to hurt you or our families—but I feel it is time to write about my feelings and knowledge.

When I was eighteen years old and going into the Navy, dad called me for a father and son talk. At that time, he told me about you being his son and how thankful he was that his brother Phil wanted to take you to love and raise. He was so pleased as he would be able to see you raised. Dad loved you, Phil, and was very proud of you and during the war worried about you. He felt sad that he was not able to raise you and tell of his love but he was so happy Phil and Clara could have you.

Dad promised Phil that he would never tell others that you were his son. I'm glad you are my brother. My children know that we are brothers.

Dad was a really good person and I wish that you could have known him as I did. I will never mention this again if you prefer me not to but I know that you know and I felt I needed you to know that I know.

I hope that you, Valerie, Linda, Bill are all great. Our family is fine. We have a good life. If you ever come to Eastern Oregon, please stop by and say Hello!!!!

My best to you and your family.

Sandy

CHAPTER 19

Final Retirement

◆◆◆◆

After his retirement from the military in 1964, Philip and his family left Kansas City and headed west. With his Army career, the family saw much of the country and decided to settle in Oregon because of its hunting, fishing, and other outdoor activities. They had a new Bonneville convertible and a new Brittany Spaniel. His mother, now aunt, went with them and continued to live with them until her death at the age of ninety-six.

They visited Medford and Eugene and finally decided to live in Salem, Oregon. Philip started hunting for a job and Valerie started hunting for a house. She found a house that was offered for sale at $45,000, but they got it for $28,000. The split-level 4,000 square foot house allowed each of the children and *grandma* to have their own bedroom and plenty of space for their hobbies.

It wasn't long before the house began to resemble a museum. Philip resurrected his taxidermy skills learned during his youth and mounted bobcats, foxes, mink, duck, pheasants, and other species of birds. His son, Bill, shot a deer at the age of thirteen and asked his dad if he could mount it. Philip wasn't sure if he could do it, but succeeded. Because of his love for wildlife and nature, Philip immersed himself into creative projects related to that theme. He enjoyed working with wood and made woodcarvings of wild birds and other scenes from nature. Philip had learned how to identify mushrooms while living in Kansas City, so he began making ceramic models of those mushrooms the family found in the Willamette Valley. He also created cross-stitch pictures of his favorite subjects.

Philip's first job was the role of a housefather at a girl's reform school. He enjoyed the job, but worked there for only two years because of the long hours that left very little time with his family.

His next job was with the City of Salem where he stayed for fifteen years. His original position was to control licenses of certain businesses. He took control of the lax status of collections, and in one year brought in more than $55,000. Although it wasn't planned, he became the city's official complaint department. If there were any shady business transactions going on in Salem, he was the one who heard about them. After several years, he became the parking supervisor and managed the meter maids and money from tickets and parking meters. He poured over the books and found there was $250,000 in delinquent parking ticket fines to the city. He took a tough stand on violators and with some detective work, found many of the culprits and collected the fines.

While he was working for the City of Salem, he was also writing for the *Capital Journal*, an outdoor writing column. During the time he lived in Kansas City, he wrote for the *Kansas City Star* and the *Fur-Fish Game,* a national magazine, so he had some experience. He wrote weekly articles about fishing, hunting, nature and even did an article on belly dancing. It seemed that belly dancing was the newest indoor-outdoor sport at the time.

After Philip's final retirement at the age of sixty-two, he bought an Avian travel trailer. By 1969, the children had left the nest so Philip and Valerie started traveling and enjoying life. During their military years, they had become accustomed to traveling, and appreciated the opportunity of being able to experience different parts of the country as well as Europe. They decided they wanted to live in a warmer climate during the winter months, so they became *snow birds,* and for fifteen years, made their annual trip to Arizona for their three-to-four-month sojourn. Philip and Valerie were always together. They were fishing and hunting companions, and were seldom without their dog Freckles. For more than twenty years, they made pine needle baskets that they sold at craft shows.

Though Philip and Valerie only knew each other for a few days back in 1943, they loved their life together and felt they had a good life. They were together for sixty-two years and four days. Sadly, Valerie, at the age of eighty-eight, was diagnosed with cancer in early September of 2005. Philip lost the love of his life three weeks later, four days after their sixty-second wedding anniversary.

EPILOGUE

Presently in this new year of 2017, Philip Edward Bishop lives in a pleasant retirement home in the state of Oregon. His Cavalier King Charles spaniel dog, Yeti, is always by his side, and they enjoy their daily walks together. Philip said if it weren't for his dog, he wouldn't be getting any exercise.

His three children all live within driving distance. One daughter lives in Washington State, and his son and other daughter live nearby in Oregon. Philip never remarried after his wife passed on.

Philip is following in his grandfather's footsteps. As quoted earlier in this book, he said, "A lifetime that spans a century is more than the number of years allowed to most men, but my grandfather lived to be one hundred years of age." This year of 2017 is Philip's year to become a true Centenarian.

✧ ✧✧

"The years teach much which the days never knew."

~ Ralph Waldo Emerson

Philip with his dog Yeti - Salem, Oregon, October, 2016

ACKNOWLEDGEMENTS

✦✦✦✦

It was such an honor to meet and interview ninety-nine-year-old World War II veteran, Philip Bishop. Writing and publishing this book, *Ever A Soldier*, about his life story is my way of thanking him for his service to our country. I appreciate the time he spent with me.

I also want to thank his daughter, Linda Bishop, for providing me with personal information and always being available to answer questions.

Thank you to my husband, who with his Army background, provided valuable insight and input about all things military in this book.

A big thank you goes to my daughter, Alecia, and my sister, June, for their loyal support and input during the first and final draft process.

And finally, to my daughter, Vivi Anne, using her talent and skills to not only format this book, but to design and create the book cover.

I feel fortunate to be surrounded by such a talented and supportive family group.

REFERENCES

✦✦✦✦

Adrian Lee. "Hitler's Last Day." *Express* 21 Jan. 2016: 1. Print.

Biography.com Editors. "Adolf Hitler Biography." *The Biography.com website*. N.p., n.d. Web. 7 Mar. 2017.

Clive Freeman. "German Castle Available-for The Right Price." *Chicago Tribune* 11 June 1995. Web. 13 Dec. 2016.

Cornish Pump and Mining Museum. "The CG-4A Glider." *Exploring The North, Inc.* N.p., n.d. Web. 7 Mar. 2017.

David P. Colley. *The Road To Victory: The Untold Story of World War II's Red Ball Express*. Warner Books Edition, 2001. Print.

History.com Staff. "World War I History." *History.com*. N.p., 2009. Web. 7 Mar. 2017.

Ken Hechler. *The Bridge at Remagen: A Story of World War II (Presidio War Classic; World War II*. Presidio Press, 2005. Print.

Nugent, T.K., and Martin Ridge. *The American West*. Indiana University Press, 1999. Web. 6 Mar. 2017.

"Office of The Historian." n. pag. Web. U.S. Entry into World War I, 1917.

Rickie Lazzerini. "The History of Idaho." (2005): 4. Print.

Robert Child. *Silent Wings- The American Glider Pilots of WWII*. Janson Media, 2013. Print.

Syd Albright. "Idaho Rides Out The Great Depression - It Wasn't Easy." *Coeur d'Alene/Post Falls Press* 27 Oct. 2013: 1. Print.

Zimowsky. "Hells Canyon: Exploring the Deepest Gorge in North America." RootsRated. N.p., 18 Feb. 2016. Web. 15 Jan. 2017.

ABOUT THE AUTHOR

Lilly Robbins Brock and her husband live in a quiet country coastal setting on the Columbia River. She began her business as an interior designer in 1980, and has recently retired. Living in the country is the ideal environment for Lilly to pursue her lifelong desire to write. She also enjoys gardening, and realized her pioneer family's planter blood is alive and well within her. Her book, *Food Gift Recipes From Nature's Bounty* was inspired by the garden and orchard. Preserving the food evolved into the idea of sharing some of that food—the gift of food.

Lilly loves history and one of her passions has been researching the genealogy of her family. She was born and raised in Olympia, Washington where her pioneer family homesteaded in the late 1800s. She has been working on a historical fiction novel, *Intrepid Journey*, about a family in the 1850s traveling on a paddle wheel steamship from New York to the rugged Pacific Northwest via the dangerous South American route. It's a revealing glimpse into the past of what life was like at that time.

Her book, *Intrepid Journey*, was put on hold when she discovered two letters written by her now deceased father while he was on the battlefront of World War II. The letters inspired her to find a World War II veteran still living and tell his story. She found her veteran and wrote *Wooden Boats & Iron Men* to honor him and all veterans.

She has now written a second World War II veteran's story in her book, *Ever A Soldier*.

Lilly feels that every veteran has a story, and at least she has been able to shine a light on these two extraordinary men.

To stay tuned in to current and upcoming projects, please feel free to visit www.lillyrobbinsbrock.com, or if you have any questions or comments, you may contact her at lillybrock62@gmail.com.

Thank you for reading this book. If you enjoyed this book, please consider leaving a short review on Amazon.com.

68927497R00076

Manufactured by Amazon.com
Columbia, SC
03 April 2017